Beyond the Will
A Comprehensive Guide to Probate Real Estate in Illinois

Dick Barr, CRS

Dedication

To my wife, Holly—your unwavering support, patience, and love have been my foundation. Thank you for your countless sacrifices and for always believing in me. This journey would not have been possible without you by my side.

To the families navigating probate, who face loss with courage and resilience. May this book serve as a guide and a source of clarity during a challenging time.

And to everyone who has trusted me to help them through their own probate journey—this book is dedicated to you.

Table of Contents:

Introduction

Your Guide to Navigating Probate Real Estate in Illinois: Practical Solutions from a Certified Residential Real Estate Probate Specialist

The probate process often arrives in our lives without warning, placing us in a position we never anticipated. When a loved one passes away, families are left to manage a range of details and emotions, all while confronting legal and financial responsibilities they may have little experience with. Probate—the court-supervised transfer of a person's assets after death—can feel like a complex maze, especially when real estate is involved. This is even more true in Illinois, where state-specific laws, rules, and terminology add layers of complexity that can be difficult to navigate without prior experience.

If you're reading this, chances are you've been tasked with responsibilities that you didn't plan for or expect. You may feel thrust into a position where you need to make important decisions without clear guidance, all while dealing with the emotional challenges that accompany loss. That's why this book exists. It's here to provide clarity, practical advice, and support at each step, to help you understand not only the process but also your options, so you can make choices that are in the best interests of you and your family.

This book approaches probate from a practical, real-world perspective. I'm a real estate broker, not an attorney, and my focus is on helping you manage the tangible aspects of probate real estate in Illinois. From securing and maintaining property during probate to understanding when and how to sell a probate property, my goal is to make these topics clear, manageable, and even empowering. This isn't a legal textbook, and it's not intended to replace the advice of an attorney. Rather, it's a practical guide rooted in years of experience, filled with insights into the probate process that you might not find elsewhere.

Throughout my career, I've worked with countless families who were facing probate for the first time. Many were overwhelmed by the Illinois-specific rules and regulations they encountered, and unsure how to move forward without risking the value of the estate or getting entangled in a long, difficult process. My hope is that this book will offer you the guidance and confidence to take control of probate real estate in a way that's informed and intentional. It's a step-by-step guide designed to make each phase—from inventorying assets to managing family dynamics—less intimidating, while providing you with insights you can rely on.

At the same time, this book is also here to support you in looking forward. Probate is a process that most people only encounter once it becomes necessary, but there are ways to prepare your own estate that can greatly simplify probate for your loved ones in the future. In the final chapters, we'll discuss practical strategies for organizing and planning your estate so that the probate process is less burdensome for those you leave behind. With the right tools, you can take steps now to protect your family from many of the difficulties that people often experience during probate.

Whether you're reading this book to manage probate real estate today, or to plan for your own future, my hope is that it will be a valuable resource for both situations. Probate can be complex, but with practical guidance and preparation, you can navigate it with confidence and make choices that best serve your family's interests. Let's begin this journey together.

Who I Am and Why I Wrote This Book

My name is Dick Barr, and I've spent much of my life helping families navigate the complex terrain of real estate transactions, imcluding those tied to probate. I'm a Managing Broker and a Certified Residential Real Estate Probate Specialist, a designation that allows me to help families facing probate with a deep, specialized understanding of what's involved in managing probate real estate. Over my career, I've worked closely with countless Illinois families who, often unexpectedly, found themselves needing to handle a loved one's estate.

Probate real estate is rarely something people plan for or expect to manage, and when you're also dealing with the loss of someone close, it can feel particularly overwhelming. My role has always been to simplify this process and guide families through each decision with practical, real-world advice that makes a difficult journey just a bit easier.

I came into this field with a passion for real estate, but over time, I found my calling in helping people through probate. Each family I've worked with has had unique needs, circumstances, and emotions tied to the process, and my aim has always been to bring compassion and clarity to each situation. As a real estate broker, I'm not just focused on transactions or market values; I'm here to help people preserve what matters most, both financially and emotionally, during a time when they need trusted support. This book is an extension of that commitment, written to provide readers with the tools, insights, and guidance that I would offer in person if we were sitting down together to discuss their probate real estate needs.

In addition to my career in real estate, I've also had the privilege of serving as a member of the Lake County Board. This role has allowed me to work on a broader level to support our communities, build relationships with trusted professionals across legal and financial fields, and deepen my understanding of the challenges that Illinois families face. My time on the Board reinforced my belief that people should have access to straightforward, reliable information, especially when it comes to the often-confusing process of probate. Through these connections and my public service, I've amassed a network of resources and professional contacts who understand Illinois probate law and share my commitment to serving our community. This experience has given me insights and access that I bring to every case and, now, to every page of this book.

Writing this book felt like a natural next step—a way to extend my reach and help more people than I could ever assist individually. Too often, I see families thrust into probate without any preparation, facing a legal system that feels foreign and complicated. In Illinois, probate comes with specific rules and steps that can be overwhelming if you don't have a roadmap, especially when real estate is involved. By sharing the knowledge I've gathered over the years, I hope to demystify this process, empowering you with clear information and practical steps that make probate more manageable.

At the same time, my goal is to help readers plan for their own futures. I want you to know that probate doesn't have to be a surprise, and there are ways to structure your own estate that make this process easier for the next generation. In this book, we'll cover steps you can take now to minimize probate requirements or even avoid them altogether for some assets. I believe that everyone deserves the peace of mind that comes with knowing their family won't be left struggling with a lengthy, stressful probate process.

In short, I wrote this book to offer you practical solutions, informed by years of hands-on experience, specialized knowledge as a Certified Real Estate Probate Specialist, and a deep commitment to serving families in Illinois. Whether you're managing a probate process now or planning for the future, I want you to have a resource that provides both guidance and reassurance. Probate real estate can be complex, but with the right support, it's a process that you can navigate successfully. Thank you for allowing me to be part of this journey with you.

Who, Not How

As much as this book is about navigating probate, it's also about recognizing the power of having the right people by your side. I believe in the philosophy of "Who, Not How," a concept from the book of the same name by Dan Sullivan. This book was gifted to me by my tax accountant, and it was truly life-changing. Sullivan's idea is simple yet profound: rather than spending precious time figuring out how to do something you may only need to do once, it's far more effective and efficient to find the right expert who already knows how to do it. "Who, Not How" fundamentally shifted how I approach challenges, teaching me that the right professional can achieve better, faster, and stronger outcomes while freeing up time for the things that matter most to me—like being with my family and building my business.

I've come to see how essential this concept is in probate, where families often try to handle everything themselves, only to find themselves overwhelmed and overextended. When facing probate, it's incredibly valuable to have a team of trusted professionals who specialize in their respective areas. Probate real estate requires knowledge of specific laws, complex financial decisions, and often emotional considerations. That's why I wrote this book with an emphasis on working with qualified experts—whether that's a probate real estate specialist, an experienced attorney, a financial advisor, or even a tax accountant. My Certified Residential Real Estate Probate Specialist designation means I've invested in specialized training to help families like yours. I can focus on what I do best, which is to simplify and streamline the real estate side of probate, while other professionals address their areas of expertise.

Throughout this book, I'll reference "Who, Not How" and the value of seeking out specialists to support you in areas that go beyond your own expertise. When we choose the right "Whos," we give ourselves a greater chance of success and peace of mind, knowing each part of the process is being handled by someone who understands it deeply. I've seen firsthand how this approach improves outcomes in probate, making the journey smoother, more efficient, and ultimately more satisfying. It's about respecting your time, protecting your family's legacy, and letting experts handle the details so you can focus on what matters most.

With the "Who, Not How" mindset, probate can feel less like a maze and more like a guided journey. Each chapter in this book will introduce the critical steps and decisions, and when specialized support is beneficial, I'll point that out. I hope you'll find value in working with the right people along the way, making probate as manageable and effective as possible—without sacrificing your time, your energy, or your peace of mind.

Why Illinois Probate Is Unique

Every state has its own rules for handling probate, but Illinois follows a particular set of statutes and procedures that create a probate landscape unlike any other. If you've heard about probate in general terms, or even if you've experienced probate in another state, you may find yourself surprised by some of the requirements in Illinois. For example, Illinois has specific steps for everything from filing initial documents to distributing assets, and these are designed to ensure that the transfer of property and other assets is legally sound. These requirements can feel overwhelming for someone without experience in probate, but understanding Illinois-specific rules can make the difference between a streamlined process and one that's drawn-out, costly, and stressful.

One of the key elements of Illinois probate is **Article VI of the Illinois Probate Statute**, which lays out essential rules for managing and distributing estate assets, including real estate. Article VI specifies how executors and administrators must handle everything from asset appraisals to creditor claims. Understanding this statute is critical for anyone involved in probate real estate because it provides the framework for what is legally required—and what happens if certain steps are missed. Throughout this book, we'll refer back to Article VI as a guide for the specific steps you'll need to take to manage probate real estate effectively.

There are three main reasons why knowing Illinois probate rules is crucial if you're involved in probate real estate:

1. **Ensuring Compliance with State Law**: Illinois probate law has specific guidelines and deadlines, particularly for valuing real estate, managing creditors, and distributing assets among heirs. Missing a deadline or skipping a required step can lead to costly delays and even legal challenges. Following Illinois' unique rules isn't just a matter of filling out forms; it's about adhering to a set of legal procedures that have been designed to ensure a fair, transparent process for all parties involved. If you're new to probate or feeling uncertain about these requirements, this book will serve as a reliable resource to help you stay on track.

2. **Protecting the Value of Real Estate Assets**: Real estate is often one of the most valuable assets in an estate, and in Illinois, it requires special care. Probate properties can lose value if they're not properly maintained or if they're left on the market too long, which is why it's important to understand how Illinois law affects these decisions. Illinois probate statutes provide guidance on issues like appraisals and disclosure

requirements, helping to preserve the property's value throughout the probate process. By understanding these guidelines, you can avoid common pitfalls that can decrease the value of the property and ultimately affect the assets passed on to heirs.

3. **Saving Time and Reducing Costs**: Probate can be notorious for taking time, but in Illinois, the process can vary greatly depending on how it's managed. By following Illinois' specific rules, you can reduce delays and even minimize expenses associated with probate. For instance, certain Illinois rules allow for simplified probate in estates under a certain value, which can reduce both time and cost. Understanding these unique options gives you greater control over the process, so you can make informed decisions that not only save you time but also reduce legal and administrative fees.

Illinois probate may feel unfamiliar and complex at first, but once you understand these foundational principles, it becomes far more manageable. With the right information, you'll be equipped to protect your family's assets, save time, and ensure a smoother process for all involved.

In addition to Illinois' specific legal requirements, probate here is also shaped by local practices and community expectations. From Lake County to Cook County and beyond, probate courts may vary in their approach, and it's important to understand these differences to avoid unnecessary surprises. As a real estate broker, I've worked closely with Illinois probate courts and developed a network of trusted contacts throughout the state. This background allows me to offer insights that go beyond standard advice, sharing practical knowledge that reflects real experiences with Illinois-specific probate real estate.

This book will help you navigate the specific requirements in Illinois, translating the legal language of the Illinois Probate Statute into clear, practical steps. From handling initial filings to preparing a property for sale, my goal is to make sure you have a solid understanding of what's needed, so you're always moving forward with confidence. We'll cover the essential requirements for managing and valuing real estate, offer tips for handling creditor claims, and discuss Illinois-specific disclosure obligations when it's time to sell a property.

The more familiar you become with Illinois probate rules, the better prepared you'll be to avoid common roadblocks and move through probate efficiently. While this guide will provide a thorough overview, remember that complex cases may benefit from additional support. Whether it's a probate attorney or a seasoned real estate broker, having professionals who understand Illinois probate law can make an invaluable difference. I'm here to provide you with the tools and information you need to navigate the process as smoothly as possible, empowering you to manage probate real estate in Illinois with confidence and clarity.

A Practical Guide from a Real Estate Perspective

When families face probate, especially for the first time, they often find themselves looking for straightforward, reliable information to help make sense of what's required of them. While there are legal and financial aspects of probate that require the expertise of attorneys and other professionals, my role as a real estate broker is to help families manage the practical aspects of probate real estate with clarity and support. This book is designed to be a practical guide from a real estate perspective, aimed at simplifying each step in managing probate property in Illinois.

As a real estate broker—not an attorney—my goal here is to provide actionable, experience-driven advice to help you navigate the day-to-day aspects of probate real estate. I bring a unique perspective that focuses on the logistical and practical challenges families encounter, whether that's deciding whether to keep or sell a property, managing property upkeep during probate, or preparing a home for the market. My goal isn't to overwhelm you with legal terminology or theory; instead, I want to offer straightforward, grounded insights that can empower you to make informed decisions at each stage.

Over my career, I've seen firsthand how complex and emotionally challenging probate can be, particularly when real estate is involved. Families are often left wondering how to secure a property, how to get an accurate appraisal, or whether a sale is in the family's best interest. These are the kinds of real-life, practical questions that I address in this book. Probate real estate requires more than just legal know-how; it demands an understanding of the local market, knowledge of the Illinois real estate landscape, and a clear approach to handling assets that may hold both sentimental and financial value. My background in real estate has equipped me to address these issues from a hands-on, actionable perspective.

The guidance in this book reflects my years of experience in Illinois real estate, where I've handled countless probate transactions for families who, in many cases, were dealing with the process for the first time. My aim is to bring the same clarity and reassurance I offer in one-on-one consultations to the pages of this book, so you feel equipped to handle the practical realities of probate with confidence. From understanding Illinois-specific disclosure requirements to learning the best ways to preserve a property's value while it's in probate, my focus is on providing tools that allow you to make decisions with confidence and clarity.

As a broker, my approach is solution-oriented. This guide is built on a foundation of tried-and-true strategies that have helped other families navigate Illinois probate real estate effectively. It's about sharing real-world, practical knowledge that reflects my time working with attorneys, appraisers, and other professionals involved in the probate process. The focus is not only on meeting legal requirements but also on helping you manage the property in a way that preserves its value, reduces stress, and respects the legacy of your loved one.

In Illinois, real estate in probate requires unique attention, especially when it comes to preparing it for sale or managing it over an extended period. Probate can often take months or even longer, and during that time, properties need to be maintained, secured, and sometimes improved. This is an area where my experience as a broker becomes particularly useful. I'll share insights on everything from managing utility payments to finding reliable service providers to ensure that the property remains well-maintained throughout the process. We'll discuss strategies for working with contractors and local resources so you can focus on what matters most, knowing that the property is in good hands.

It's also worth noting that probate properties come with specific disclosure requirements in Illinois, which can sometimes catch families by surprise. This book will prepare you for those requirements, explaining what needs to be disclosed when selling a probate property, how to handle potential repairs, and what buyers typically look for in these cases. I'll offer guidance on pricing and marketing strategies that fit the unique needs of probate properties, so that when the time comes to sell, you can do so with confidence and peace of mind.

While this guide will provide comprehensive information, some cases may benefit from additional professional support. If you have legal questions or more complex probate issues, I encourage you to consult with an Illinois probate attorney who can offer specific advice tailored to your case. I've also included guidance on choosing a probate attorney or financial advisor, if you feel that additional expertise would be beneficial. My role here is to offer the practical, actionable advice that will support you on a daily basis, empowering you to move through the probate real estate process with as much ease as possible.

At the end of the day, probate real estate is about more than just handling property—it's about honoring your loved one's legacy and making thoughtful decisions for the future. My hope is that this guide will give you the clarity, tools, and reassurance you need to feel well-prepared at each step, from securing the property to finalizing its sale or distribution. You may be facing unfamiliar territory, but with the right guidance, you can take control of the process and approach it with confidence.

Planning for the Future: Minimizing the Burdens of Probate

While probate is often something families encounter unexpectedly, the truth is that there are ways to prepare for it ahead of time. In fact, some of the most effective probate strategies are those put into place well before they're needed. Whether you're currently navigating probate for a loved one or planning ahead to ensure your own estate is managed smoothly in the future, this book offers tools and insights that can make a real difference. While it's common to feel like probate is something "thrust upon" you, I want you to know that it doesn't have to be that way for future generations.

One of the most valuable aspects of this book is its dual purpose: it's designed not only to help you manage a probate process if you're going through one now but also to offer actionable planning strategies for those looking to ease the burden of probate on their own families. With the right planning, you can simplify the probate process for your loved ones, reducing delays, preserving the value of assets, and avoiding many of the common challenges people encounter. By taking certain steps now, you can give your family peace of mind, knowing that when the time comes, they'll be prepared.

There are several ways to plan your estate to reduce the impact of probate on your heirs. Some of these strategies allow you to transfer assets directly without going through probate at all, while others simply help streamline the process, making it easier and faster for your family. We'll cover practical tools like **transfer-on-death deeds**, which allow you to designate a beneficiary for real estate, and **trusts**, which provide ways to transfer assets without probate oversight. These options can significantly reduce the time, costs, and legal requirements involved in managing an estate, and they're strategies that anyone can implement with the right guidance.

In addition to asset-transfer tools, proper estate planning involves organizing documentation, selecting reliable executors or trustees, and making key decisions ahead of time about how your assets should be handled. The more clarity you can provide now, the less room there is for confusion or disagreement later. Throughout this book, I'll outline ways you can organize your estate to make sure everything is in order for your loved ones. From creating a comprehensive list of assets to keeping essential documents in one accessible place, small actions today can make an enormous difference in the probate process tomorrow.

One of the most impactful steps you can take to plan for the future is simply to communicate your wishes clearly. Too often, families enter probate with little to no understanding of their loved one's intentions or plans. By talking to your family about your estate and your desires for how it should be managed, you help eliminate potential misunderstandings and avoid family disputes that can slow down probate and create unnecessary stress. We'll go over ways to approach these conversations, making sure that they're as smooth and constructive as possible.

Planning for probate doesn't have to be overwhelming, and taking even small steps now can provide your family with a sense of security and clarity down the road. For many people, the thought of planning for probate can seem daunting, but I want to assure you that these strategies are not only manageable, they're empowering. By addressing probate needs in advance, you're creating a legacy that provides for your family in the best way possible, sparing them the stress and unknowns that come when probate planning is left to chance.

This book is designed to be your guide through both scenarios: helping you navigate the probate process if you're facing it now, and giving you the tools to proactively protect your family in the future. While probate can feel intimidating, the right planning puts you in control of the process, ensuring that your assets are managed according to your wishes and that your family is prepared. Together, we'll explore not only what's required during probate but also how you can prepare your own estate to minimize these requirements for those who come after you.

Estate planning is a personal process, and it should reflect your values, priorities, and intentions. I'll share tips for making sure your wishes are clearly documented, organized, and legally protected, so your estate plan is both effective and aligned with your goals. While no one can foresee every future event, planning for probate is about providing peace of mind and a clear path forward for your loved ones. My hope is that this book becomes a lasting resource, something you can turn to whenever you're ready to start planning or revisit your current plans.

By the end of this book, you'll have a comprehensive understanding of the Illinois probate process, along with strategies you can use to reduce or even eliminate probate burdens for your family. You'll have practical knowledge and tools at your disposal—whether you're navigating probate today or preparing for the future. With the right planning, probate doesn't have to be an obstacle; instead, it can be an organized, predictable process that ensures your legacy is passed on smoothly, just as you intended.

How to Use This Book

Navigating probate real estate is rarely straightforward, and it can be overwhelming to know where to start. This book is designed to be a comprehensive guide to the probate process as it relates to real estate in Illinois, offering clear explanations, practical steps, and actionable insights that you can rely on as you go through each stage. Whether you're just starting the probate process for a loved one's estate, dealing with a specific probate challenge, or looking to plan ahead to make things easier for your family, this book is here to serve as a trusted resource.

Each chapter builds on the last, taking you step-by-step through everything from the basics of probate to advanced planning strategies. You can read this book cover to cover, following each chapter in sequence as you move through the probate process, or you can skip to specific sections if you're looking for guidance on a particular issue. It's structured to offer flexibility, so you can use it in the way that best meets your needs.

Throughout each chapter, I've included real-life examples, practical checklists, and easy-to-follow steps that can help simplify even the most complex probate topics. You'll also find tips for managing some of the common emotional and logistical challenges people face during probate—whether that's finding a reliable appraiser, securing a vacant property, or talking to family members about difficult topics. Each section is designed to give you hands-on tools and insights that make a real difference in the probate process.

Additionally, the book includes a **glossary of terms** at the back where you can quickly reference definitions or find answers to common questions. Probate is full of terminology that can feel overwhelming at first, and these resources are here to help make the language of probate more accessible, so you don't get bogged down in technical jargon.

This book is here to serve you, whether you're facing probate right now or planning for your family's future. My hope is that you'll find the guidance you need to move forward with clarity, confidence, and peace of mind. Some readers may find it helpful to consult the entire book as a comprehensive guide, while others may want to focus on a specific area that applies to their immediate needs. Probate can be a journey, and I've designed this book to meet you wherever you are on that path, giving you the flexibility to use it in the way that best suits you.

Ultimately, this book is about making probate more manageable. It's written to offer support at every step, from the initial stages of probate to closing the estate, and from practical tools for today to forward-looking strategies that will help your loved ones tomorrow. Probate doesn't have to be intimidating, and with the right guidance, you'll have a clear path through it. Thank you for allowing me to share this knowledge with you, and I hope this guide becomes a helpful companion as you navigate the probate process or prepare for the future.

Moving Forward, One Step at a Time

Entering the probate process can feel like stepping into unfamiliar territory, filled with legal terms, rules, and responsibilities that most people have never encountered before. And when you add the emotional weight of losing a loved one, it's no wonder that many families feel overwhelmed. If you're feeling uncertain or even anxious about probate, I want to reassure you: you're not alone in this, and it's perfectly normal to feel this way. Probate can be challenging, but it's a process that, with the right support, can be manageable—and even empowering.

This book is structured to guide you through each part of probate real estate in Illinois, breaking down every step into manageable, easy-to-understand pieces. My goal is to walk you through the complexities of probate one step at a time, so you never feel lost or unsure about what comes next. With clear explanations, practical tips, and Illinois-specific guidance, you'll gain the tools and confidence you need to make informed decisions for your family. I know that each decision in probate matters, and this guide is here to help you make those choices with clarity and purpose.

Navigating probate isn't just about following legal requirements; it's also about honoring your loved one's legacy and making sure their wishes are respected. This can bring an added sense of responsibility and even stress, especially if you're handling an estate that has personal significance or emotional ties for you and your family. Probate is often as much an emotional journey as it is a legal one, and it's normal to experience a range of emotions along the way. As you move through the process, remember to take it one step at a time, allowing yourself the space to make thoughtful, well-informed choices. Each chapter in this book is crafted to provide you with insights that support you, both practically and emotionally.

If you're just beginning the probate process, know that it's okay to take things slowly and ask questions. Probate is a step-by-step process, and each phase builds on the last. This book will help you approach it systematically, so that no step feels overwhelming or rushed. As you move forward, use the chapters to guide your actions, from securing the property to handling appraisals, managing family dynamics, and eventually closing the estate. While each probate case is unique, this book will provide a solid foundation that can help you navigate even the unexpected challenges that may arise.

And if you're reading this book as part of your estate planning, remember that taking steps now to prepare your own estate is one of the most meaningful things you can do for your family. Planning ahead allows you to take control of the process, ensuring that your estate is handled according to your wishes and that your loved ones are protected from the stresses of probate. Estate planning is an empowering act, one that creates a smoother, more secure path for those who will manage your estate in the future. This book will help you not only navigate probate but also create a legacy that reflects your values and priorities.

Throughout this guide, I've included real-life examples, practical tips, and insights based on years of experience in Illinois probate real estate. These elements are designed to make each step of the process more approachable, breaking down complicated issues into understandable parts. You'll find checklists to keep you organized, suggestions for handling common obstacles, and advice for choosing the right professionals to support you. Probate may have its challenges, but you don't have to face them alone or unprepared. This book is here to be a companion, offering support every step of the way.

As you go through this book, remember that probate isn't something you need to "master" overnight. Each step is a chance to learn, adapt, and make decisions that are best for you and your family. And with each chapter, you'll gain a clearer understanding of what needs to be done, why it matters, and how to do it in a way that aligns with your goals and values. This process is about moving forward, even if it's just one step at a time.

Finally, know that it's perfectly okay to seek additional support along the way. Probate can be complex, and every case has its own unique circumstances. This book provides a thorough guide, but there may be times when consulting an attorney, financial advisor, or experienced real estate broker can make a significant difference. Don't hesitate to reach out when you need it—building a reliable team can be one of the best decisions you make for your family.

In the end, probate is a journey, but it doesn't have to be overwhelming. With the right information and a clear path, you can take control of the process, navigate each stage with confidence, and make choices that honor your loved one's memory. Whether you're managing probate today or planning for the future, I hope this book becomes a valuable resource, offering you the guidance, reassurance, and clarity to move forward with peace of mind. Thank you for allowing me to be a part of this journey with you. Now, let's take it one step at a time, together.

Chapter 1

Understanding Probate Basics in Illinois

Navigating probate can be challenging, especially when real estate is involved. Probate is a court-supervised process that ensures a deceased person's assets are legally transferred to heirs or beneficiaries, providing a structured approach to settling debts and distributing property. In Illinois, specific laws govern the probate process, which affects how real estate is handled, who receives ownership, and how assets are legally protected. In this chapter, we'll cover the fundamentals of probate, explain why it's necessary for real estate transfers, and break down the types of assets that may or may not require probate. By understanding these basics, you'll be well-prepared for the steps ahead in managing or planning for probate real estate.

What Is Probate?

When a person passes away, their property, finances, and other assets collectively form what's known as an *estate*. While many people focus on the value or sentimental meaning of their assets, fewer anticipate the legal steps required to properly transfer these items to their intended heirs. That's where probate comes into play.

Probate is a court-supervised process that helps ensure an orderly and legal transfer of assets after someone dies. It is designed to prevent misunderstandings, unauthorized claims, and disputes by creating a structured pathway for managing the estate. Probate not only ensures that any debts and taxes owed by the deceased are paid but also makes sure that any remaining assets are distributed according to the deceased's wishes—or, if there's no will, according to Illinois state law. Probate is the court's method for ensuring that everything is handled fairly and accurately, while also providing a framework to resolve any conflicts.

Probate can be thought of as a series of checks and balances. First, the court verifies whether there's a will and determines whether it's valid. This verification step is essential; without it, the risk of fraud or conflict rises significantly. Probate also appoints someone to manage the estate—this person is known as the *executor* if there is a will, or the *administrator* if there isn't one. The executor or administrator plays a vital role, responsible for gathering and valuing assets, notifying creditors, paying debts, and eventually distributing property to heirs or beneficiaries.

Consider a scenario: a loved one has passed away and left behind a home, a retirement account, a bank account, personal belongings, and some unpaid bills. Probate will oversee the process of ensuring that these assets and obligations are handled according to the law. The court will require the executor to inventory each asset, settle any debts or taxes, and, finally, distribute the remaining property. While this process can feel like extra work, especially when grieving, probate exists to provide protections that ensure fairness and respect for everyone involved.

Why Probate Matters

For families, probate can sometimes feel like an unnecessary formality. It can appear to be a process that simply adds more steps during an already difficult time. However, probate serves important purposes to safeguard the estate, protect beneficiaries, and ensure creditors are treated fairly. Without probate, disputes over assets could easily arise, creditors might come after heirs if debts were unpaid, and families could face lingering legal and financial complications.

In Illinois, probate serves several critical functions to prevent these complications and protect all parties involved, including:

- **Guarding Against Unpaid Debts**: Probate provides a court-supervised method for settling debts. Without this, creditors could potentially pursue heirs directly for what they're owed. By requiring debts to be paid first, probate ensures that heirs receive their inheritance free from outstanding obligations.

- **Providing a Structured Dispute Resolution Process**: Families can often experience disagreements during probate, especially if there are differing interpretations of the will or disputes over certain assets. Probate allows the court to oversee these disagreements and ensures a fair, impartial resolution.

- **Protecting Executors and Beneficiaries**: The court's oversight of executors and administrators means that the estate manager must follow specific legal procedures and meet court expectations. This structured process ensures that assets are managed carefully and that all heirs and beneficiaries receive their rightful inheritance.

For Illinois families, probate brings clarity and structure to estate management, which can be especially valuable during emotionally challenging times. Knowing that the estate is managed properly—and that each step is protected by law—can give everyone involved peace of mind.

How Probate Impacts Families and Loved Ones

Probate can feel complex, especially for loved ones who are not familiar with the process. During a time of loss, family members are often faced with deadlines, court appearances, and financial requirements that they may feel unprepared for. For first-time executors or administrators, the responsibilities can feel overwhelming.

In Illinois, probate involves a number of critical responsibilities, such as notifying creditors, preparing an inventory of assets, keeping thorough records, and ensuring that all steps meet the requirements set by the court. In addition to these responsibilities, the executor must make careful financial decisions—often during an emotional time. Missteps can result in penalties, delays, and additional expenses, all of which can add to the family's stress.

Despite these challenges, probate can provide invaluable protections that ultimately bring peace of mind. Probate may require time and patience, but it protects against situations where someone might wrongfully try to claim property or where a creditor might seek more than they are entitled to. By following probate procedures, families gain reassurance that each asset is accounted for and handled fairly. Knowing that a loved one's estate is being managed according to Illinois law, with all necessary protections, helps families feel confident that they're honoring their loved one's legacy.

Illinois-Specific Probate Rules

Every state has unique probate rules, and Illinois has its own set of laws designed to protect everyone involved in an estate. In Illinois, probate is generally required if an estate's total value exceeds $100,000 or includes real estate. However, some assets can bypass probate altogether, potentially simplifying the process for certain estates.

Understanding Illinois-specific rules is key to navigating probate effectively. For instance, certain types of assets—like those held in joint ownership or accounts with beneficiary designations—can avoid probate entirely, allowing families to settle some portions of the estate more quickly. Knowing which assets require probate and which do not can give families a clearer view of the tasks ahead and may even help them bypass some steps.

In short, Illinois probate law is designed to ensure a fair, structured, and transparent process. Although it may seem complex at first, understanding Illinois probate can help families feel more in control, simplifying their responsibilities and easing the path forward.

When Does Probate Apply?

Probate doesn't always apply to every asset or every situation. Knowing when probate is required—and when it's not—can save families time, reduce legal expenses, and make the process less overwhelming. Probate typically applies only to certain types of property, especially when the assets are solely in the deceased's name and lack a designated beneficiary.

In Illinois, probate is generally required when:

- **The estate's total value exceeds $100,000.**

- **The deceased owned real estate solely in their name without co-owners or transfer-on-death designations.**

Understanding which assets need probate and which do not can help families reduce the court's involvement, allowing them to streamline the process when possible.

Types of Assets That Typically Require Probate

These are assets that don't have built-in transfer mechanisms, meaning they must go through probate to legally transfer to the heirs or beneficiaries:

1. **Real Estate Owned Solely by the Deceased**: If the deceased was the only owner of a property, probate is generally required to transfer the title to another party.

2. **Bank and Investment Accounts Without Beneficiaries**: Accounts without designated beneficiaries (such as checking or savings accounts held solely in the deceased's name) will typically go through probate.

3. **Valuable Personal Property**: Items such as valuable jewelry, art, vehicles, and other personal items that aren't jointly owned or don't have designated beneficiaries may need probate if they total more than $100,000 in value.

4. **Business Ownership**: If the deceased owned shares in a private company or had a business interest, probate may be necessary to determine ownership rights and facilitate a legal transfer of business assets.

Each of these assets requires probate to verify ownership, settle debts, and ensure proper distribution to the rightful heirs or beneficiaries.

Types of Assets That Bypass Probate

Some assets have a built-in transfer process that allows them to avoid probate, simplifying the distribution and reducing delays. These are known as *non-probate assets*, and they include:

1. **Jointly Owned Property with Rights of Survivorship**: When property is held jointly with survivorship rights—such as between spouses—it automatically transfers to the surviving owner, bypassing probate.

2. **Accounts with Beneficiary Designations**: Financial accounts like retirement accounts, life insurance policies, and certain bank accounts often allow the owner to name a beneficiary.

These accounts transfer directly to the beneficiary, avoiding probate.

3. **Transfer-on-Death (TOD) and Payable-on-Death (POD) Accounts**: Illinois allows certain accounts and assets, such as bank accounts and securities, to have a TOD or POD designation. With this setup, the accounts pass directly to the named person upon death.

4. **Assets Held in a Trust**: Assets placed in a trust are managed according to the trust's terms and, therefore, avoid probate. A trust provides privacy, flexibility, and quicker distribution of assets, making it a popular option for those looking to minimize probate.

5. **Small Estates**: Estates valued at $100,000 or less may qualify for Illinois's *Small Estate Affidavit*, a simplified option that lets heirs bypass probate under specific conditions.

Identifying non-probate assets can help families focus on the areas of the estate that truly require probate, streamlining their responsibilities and reducing court involvement where possible.

Planning Ahead to Minimize Probate

Planning ahead to minimize probate can simplify the process for loved ones, saving them time, reducing costs, and easing the stress that comes with probate requirements. By setting up assets to bypass probate, individuals can ensure that their estate transfers smoothly to heirs and reduces court involvement.

Consider these strategies for minimizing probate:

- **Establish Beneficiary Designations**: Many assets, like life insurance policies, retirement accounts, and certain bank accounts, allow you to name beneficiaries. Regularly review these designations, especially after major life changes, to make sure they're up to date. Doing so allows these assets to transfer outside of probate.

- **Use TOD and POD Designations**: Illinois allows individuals to designate beneficiaries for certain bank accounts and real estate with a *Transfer-on-Death* or *Payable-on-Death* form.

These simple designations let assets transfer immediately without probate.

- **Consider a Living Trust**: A living trust allows assets to transfer directly to beneficiaries without going through probate. This approach provides privacy and flexibility in managing assets, letting the trust terms control distribution rather than probate.

- **Use Joint Ownership for Certain Assets**: Jointly owning assets, such as a home or bank accounts, can allow these assets to transfer directly to the surviving owner, avoiding probate. This is commonly done with spouses but can apply to other co-owners.

- **Reduce the Estate Size**: If the estate value is close to or under $100,000, it may qualify for Illinois's Small Estate Affidavit process. Keeping the estate within this limit can let families bypass probate, saving both time and costs.

By preparing with these strategies in mind, families can help make probate easier or, in some cases, avoid it entirely, providing their heirs with a smoother process and preserving more of the estate for loved ones.

The Illinois Probate Court System

In Illinois, probate is managed through the circuit court system, with each county having a probate division responsible for overseeing estates of residents who passed away in that area. This local system provides an accessible venue for probate while ensuring that all estates are managed according to Illinois laws. While Illinois probate laws apply across the state, each county's probate court may have specific forms, schedules, or procedures.

For example, in larger counties like Cook or Lake, probate courts may have more formalized processes due to a higher volume of cases. In smaller counties, the courts may only hold probate hearings on certain days or have limited hours, which can impact timelines. Working with probate professionals familiar with your county's procedures can help you navigate these differences.

Roles of the Illinois Probate Court

The Illinois probate court plays several critical roles to ensure fair, transparent estate management:

1. **Validating Wills**: The probate court first verifies any will's validity, ensuring it meets Illinois's legal standards.

2. **Appointing Executors or Administrators**: If no executor is named or the designated person cannot serve, the court appoints an administrator to manage the estate according to state law.

3. **Reviewing the Asset Inventory**: Executors must submit a detailed list of assets, which the court reviews for accuracy and transparency.

4. **Handling Creditor Claims**: The court oversees creditors, allowing them to submit claims and ensuring that legitimate debts are paid from the estate's assets.

5. **Authorizing Distribution of Assets**: Once all debts are settled, the court authorizes asset distribution based on the will or Illinois's intestacy laws.

6. **Resolving Disputes**: If conflicts arise—such as challenges to the will's validity or disputes among heirs—the court serves as a neutral forum to resolve these issues legally.

Understanding the probate court's role and structure can help families navigate probate with confidence, knowing that Illinois probate courts work to ensure fairness and accountability at each step.

Navigating County-Specific Probate Differences

Each Illinois county follows statewide probate law, but local variations exist that can affect timing and requirements. Here are a few examples:

- **Forms and Documentation**: Some counties may require additional forms, while others have simpler document requirements.

- **Hearing Availability**: In busier counties, scheduling probate hearings can take longer due to higher caseloads.

- **Filing Procedures**: Some counties allow e-filing for probate cases, while others may require physical submissions.

To avoid unnecessary delays, it's helpfsul to familiarize yourself with your county's specific probate requirements or consult with local professionals.

The Probate Timeline

Probate is a step-by-step process that unfolds over months, and sometimes even longer, depending on various factors. In Illinois, probate typically takes six months to a year, though complex cases or estates with disputes may extend beyond this period.

General Stages of Probate

1. **Opening Probate** (1-3 Months): Probate begins when the executor files a petition to open the estate. Once the court approves the petition, it grants *Letters of Office*, authorizing the executor to manage the estate.

2. **Inventorying and Appraising Assets** (2-4 Months): The executor prepares a complete inventory of the estate, documenting all assets, and submits it to the court. High-value assets may require formal appraisals.

3. **Settling Debts and Taxes** (4-6 Months): The executor notifies creditors and pays any valid claims from the estate's funds. In Illinois, creditors have six months to submit claims.

4. **Distributing Remaining Assets** (1-2 Months): Once debts are paid, the executor distributes the remaining assets to beneficiaries as directed by the will or according to Illinois intestacy laws.

5. **Closing Probate** (1-3 Months): The executor files a final accounting with the court. If approved, the court closes probate, releasing the executor from their responsibilities.

By understanding these stages, families can better anticipate each phase and move through probate with greater confidence.

In Summary: Moving from Probate Basics to Practical Steps Ahead

Probate may feel intimidating at first, but understanding the basics brings clarity and confidence. With this foundation, you're better prepared to handle each step thoughtfully, honor your loved one's legacy, and face each stage of the process with clarity.

The chapters ahead will guide you through practical steps to manage Illinois probate, from handling assets and working with professionals to planning for your own future. Thank you for beginning this journey with me; together, we'll navigate each step in a way that honors your loved one's memory and protects your family's future.

Chapter 1 Summary: Key Takeaways on Probate Basics in Illinois

In Chapter 1, we covered the essentials of probate in Illinois, including its purpose, requirements, and the protections it offers families. Here are the main points readers explored in this chapter:

- **The Purpose of Probate**: Probate is a court-supervised process designed to ensure a deceased person's assets are managed and distributed according to Illinois law. By establishing legal oversight, probate helps prevent disputes, ensures debts are paid, and honors the decedent's wishes fairly.

- **Why Probate Matters for Families**: While probate may feel complex, it provides critical protections for heirs, beneficiaries, and creditors. By following probate procedures, families gain peace of mind, knowing that the estate is handled legally and equitably, minimizing the risk of conflicts or unexpected claims on the estate.

- **Illinois Probate Rules**: Probate is generally required in Illinois if an estate's value exceeds $100,000 or includes real estate. However, some assets—such as jointly owned property, accounts with beneficiaries, and assets held in trusts—bypass probate, allowing for quicker transfers and simplifying the process.

- **Types of Assets Requiring Probate**: Certain assets like real estate solely in the decedent's name, bank accounts without beneficiaries, and valuable personal property require probate to legally transfer ownership. Understanding which assets need probate helps families focus on only the portions of the estate that require court involvement.

- **Ways to Minimize Probate**: Various planning tools, such as beneficiary designations, trusts, and joint ownership, can simplify probate or, in some cases, help avoid it altogether. These strategies reduce court involvement, save time, and preserve more of the estate's value for loved ones.

- **The Illinois Probate Court System and Timeline**: Probate is handled through local circuit courts in Illinois and generally takes several months, following a structured timeline from filing the petition to closing the estate. Knowing this timeline helps families anticipate each phase of probate and prepare accordingly.

Chapter 1 provided a foundational understanding of probate's purpose, requirements, and protections. With these basics, families are better equipped to approach the probate process confidently, handling each step thoughtfully and effectively.

Checklist: Key Points for Understanding Probate
and Real Estate in Illinois

1. Understanding Probate Basics
- ☐ Familiarize yourself with what probate is: the court-supervised process of transferring a deceased person's assets to heirs or beneficiaries.
- ☐ Recognize that probate is designed to ensure fair handling of assets, payment of debts, and lawful distribution to beneficiaries.

2. Why Probate Is Needed for Real Estate
- ☐ Understand that real estate typically does not transfer automatically to heirs without probate unless specific arrangements are made (e.g., joint tenancy).
- ☐ Confirm whether the property in question requires probate by considering if it's solely in the decedent's name or if it lacks a beneficiary designation.
- ☐ Recognize the importance of probate for legally transferring ownership, especially when the property's title needs to be updated or sold.

3. Familiarize Yourself with the Illinois Probate Statute (Especially Article VI)
- ☐ Review key sections of the Illinois Probate Statute, particularly Article VI, which covers rules and procedures specific to real estate in probate.
- ☐ Understand that the Illinois Probate Statute outlines requirements for handling real estate, such as inventorying assets, notifying creditors, and managing tax liabilities.

4. Distinguish Between Probate and Non-Probate Assets
- ☐ Identify probate assets: These are assets that must go through probate because they are solely in the decedent's name without designated beneficiaries (e.g., real estate held individually, personal property, or certain bank accounts).

☐ Identify non-probate assets: These include assets that pass automatically to beneficiaries outside of probate, such as:
  ☐ Jointly-owned property with rights of survivorship.
  ☐ Payable-on-death (POD) or transfer-on-death (TOD) accounts.
  ☐ Life insurance policies with a designated beneficiary.
  ☐ Retirement accounts (e.g., IRAs or 401(k)s) with named beneficiaries.
☐ Evaluate if estate planning tools, such as trusts, joint tenancy, or beneficiary designations, can help reduce probate involvement for certain assets.

Chapter 2

Initial Steps After a Loved One's Passing

The days and weeks following a loved one's passing can be emotionally overwhelming, especially when it comes to handling their estate. For families managing real estate during probate, knowing the initial steps can help bring clarity and a sense of order. This chapter provides a practical guide to securing the property, gathering essential documents, and understanding the role of the executor or administrator in real estate matters. By addressing these early tasks, you'll lay a solid foundation for a smooth probate process, reducing stress and helping ensure the estate is managed responsibly and according to Illinois law.

Securing the Property

When a loved one passes, one of the first, often unexpected, responsibilities families face is securing the deceased's property. This process can be emotional and, for many, feels daunting, especially in a time of grief. But securing the property is a critical first step in the probate process, not only to protect it from potential risks but also to prepare it for the journey through probate.

This section provides a step-by-step guide for securing property in probate, focusing on physical, legal, and financial protections to ensure it remains in good standing. Remember, however, that while this guide outlines the general process, it's always advisable to consult with a probate lawyer or real estate professional familiar with probate properties to ensure your steps align with Illinois probate laws and best practices.

Why Securing the Property is Essential

The loss of a loved one can leave a property vulnerable. Even in safe neighborhoods, an unoccupied home can attract potential risks, from theft or vandalism to maintenance issues that can quickly spiral into larger problems. Securing the property addresses these risks head-on, reducing liability concerns and helping the executor fulfill their duty to protect and preserve the estate's assets.

In Illinois, executors and administrators—those appointed to manage the deceased's estate—are responsible for maintaining the property. This includes protecting it from damage, ensuring taxes are paid, and ultimately, preparing it for probate proceedings. Taking initial security steps immediately after the owner's passing is essential to avoid complications that may otherwise impact the estate's value or pose legal challenges during probate.

Immediate Steps for Physical Security

Change the Locks and Secure All Entry Points

One of the most immediate steps after a loved one's passing is to ensure the home is secure by changing the locks. Many families assume that only close relatives have keys to the property, but in reality, friends, neighbors, or service workers may have access. Changing locks ensures that only authorized family members and professionals can access the property, helping to prevent unauthorized entry or potential disputes later.

Additionally, if the property includes multiple entry points—such as garages, back doors, or detached storage units—these should also be secured. A probate real estate agent or property management company can assist with this process, especially if the family lives out of state or has difficulty managing these initial steps.

Set Up an Alarm System and Consider Security Monitoring

An alarm system can serve as an effective deterrent to theft or vandalism, especially for properties that will remain vacant for a prolonged period. Families may consider reactivating or installing a new security system, which can often be arranged through local security companies on a temporary or short-term basis. Many modern systems provide mobile access, allowing family members to monitor activity remotely.

Some families also find value in hiring a professional property management service, especially if the property is in a high-risk area or will remain unoccupied for months. These services can handle security checks and general maintenance, ensuring that the property remains safe and well-kept.

Notify Local Authorities of the Vacant Property

In Illinois, notifying local law enforcement that a property is vacant can be a valuable step. Many police departments provide "vacation watch" services where officers periodically check on vacant homes. Letting local authorities know about the vacancy can deter criminal activity and increase security. In some cases, local police can even offer tips for specific security measures based on neighborhood crime data.

Documenting and Inventorying Property Contents

Conduct a Thorough Walk-Through

Executors and family members should conduct an initial walk-through of the property as soon as it is secured. This walkthrough serves as an opportunity to document the property's current condition and identify any immediate maintenance or security needs. It's essential to take detailed notes and photos of each room, focusing on valuable items or areas that may require repairs.

Create an Inventory of Assets Inside the Property

Inventorying all personal belongings, furnishings, and valuables inside the home helps create a formal record, which is crucial for the probate process. In Illinois, executors are required to list all estate assets in a document called an **inventory**, which they must file with the court. Detailed records ensure transparency for all heirs and help avoid potential disputes or misunderstandings about the distribution of personal property.

To create a comprehensive inventory:

- Start with high-value items, such as jewelry, electronics, antiques, and collectibles.

- Move through the house methodically, room by room, to avoid missing any significant items.

- Consider photographing or videotaping items of value to provide additional documentation.

If the property contains high-value items, like artwork or collectibles, it's often wise to hire a professional appraiser. This ensures accurate valuation, which is essential for probate filings and can provide clarity among heirs.

Secure and Remove High-Value or Sentimental Items

In some cases, it may be best to remove valuables from the property until it is sold or transferred. This is particularly true if the property will be vacant or if there is any risk of theft. Items like jewelry, heirlooms, and sensitive documents (such as wills or financial records) should be moved to a secure location, such as a safety deposit box or a trusted family member's home.

A probate attorney or experienced executor may advise on proper procedures for handling these items, including documenting any removed assets to avoid misunderstandings later.

Handling Immediate Maintenance Needs

Address Critical Repairs or Hazards

If the home has maintenance issues that could worsen over time—such as leaking pipes, damaged roofs, or electrical problems—addressing these repairs immediately is crucial. Failure to manage essential repairs can lead to greater expenses down the line and may affect the estate's overall value. Often, executors can use estate funds to cover necessary repairs, provided they document expenses carefully.

An experienced probate real estate agent can assist in assessing necessary repairs or refer trusted contractors. However, it's crucial to avoid excessive renovations; probate properties are generally sold "as-is," and any major improvements should be discussed with a probate lawyer or real estate professional to determine if they're warranted.

Basic Maintenance for Vacant Properties

For properties that will remain unoccupied, basic maintenance is important to prevent deterioration. Routine lawn care, pest control, and occasional cleaning ensure that the property remains presentable. These tasks may seem minor, but they can make a significant difference in the property's marketability and protect its value during the probate process.

Many families find that hiring a property management service or arranging for a local caretaker is a practical solution, especially if they're located out of state or have other responsibilities. This "Who, not how" approach frees family members from hands-on management and allows professionals to keep the property in optimal condition.

Financial Security and Insurance Adjustments

Update Homeowners' Insurance

One often-overlooked aspect of securing a probate property is ensuring that the homeowners' insurance is up to date. In Illinois, standard homeowners' policies may not cover vacant properties, so it's critical to notify the insurer of the owner's passing and the property's vacancy status. In some cases, families may need to purchase a vacant home insurance policy to maintain coverage.

Failing to update insurance can leave the property vulnerable to uncovered losses in the event of theft, fire, or damage. If uncertain about the right insurance steps, family members should consult a probate attorney or insurance professional who understands probate properties.

Notify Utility Providers and Address Outstanding Bills

After securing the home, families should contact utility providers to maintain essential services (like heating in winter) and prevent service disruptions. Executors may also need to address any outstanding utility bills to avoid complications, especially if a probate sale will occur in the future. Keeping utilities running ensures that the property remains safe and marketable, especially in Illinois' cold months when vacant homes are prone to plumbing issues if left without heat.

Final Note: When to Consult a Professional

Securing the property is just the first step in a series of actions required to handle a probate property effectively. This stage, though straightforward, is often more manageable with professional support. Probate attorneys, property management companies, and probate-experienced real estate agents can help alleviate the burden on families, ensuring all steps are completed efficiently.

While securing a property may seem like something family members can handle alone, remember that probate involves significant legal and financial considerations. Consulting a probate lawyer or a probate-specific real estate agent early on provides peace of mind and ensures that the property is in capable hands.

Checklist of Professionals to Consider When Securing a Probate Property

Securing a probate property involves both physical and financial measures to protect its value and prepare it for probate proceedings. Here's a checklist of recommended professionals to consider, along with the roles they play in helping executors or administrators handle this important first step.

---

1. Locksmith
- **Purpose**: Change locks and secure all entry points to prevent unauthorized access.
- **When Needed**: Immediately after the property is vacated or upon discovering existing security risks.
- **Tip**: Consider locksmiths who can also assess additional security needs for garages, sheds, and other entry points.

2. Security System Provider
- **Purpose**: Install or reactivate an alarm system for added protection.
- **When Needed**: If the property will remain vacant or is located in a higher-risk area.
- **Tip**: Look for providers offering short-term, remote-access security plans suitable for vacant properties.

3. Property Management or Preservation Company
- **Purpose**: Manage regular upkeep, conduct security checks, and handle basic maintenance.
- **When Needed**: For out-of-state executors or properties expected to be vacant for extended periods.

- **Tip**: Seek out companies experienced in handling probate properties, especially those able to address seasonal upkeep like lawn care and snow removal.

4. Professional Cleaners
- **Purpose**: Conduct initial cleaning and, if necessary, ongoing maintenance.
- **When Needed**: Before property viewings, during the probate process, or as part of routine upkeep for a vacant property.
- **Tip**: Consider specialty cleaning services if the property requires extensive cleaning, such as post-tenant cleanup.

5. Real Estate Broker with Probate Experience
- **Purpose**: Conduct a market analysis, assist with property value assessment, and guide property sale strategies.
- **When Needed**: As early as possible if the property will be listed for sale.
- **Tip**: Look for a broker with specific experience in probate real estate to navigate unique probate sale requirements and court approvals.

6. Probate Attorney
- **Purpose**: Provide legal guidance on securing the property, filing necessary probate documents, and protecting estate assets.
- **When Needed**: Essential from the outset to ensure compliance with Illinois probate laws and to handle legal complexities.
- **Tip**: Probate attorneys can also advise on document handling, property access rights, and communication with creditors or heirs.

7. Insurance Agent Specializing in Vacant Property Policies
- **Purpose**: Update the property's insurance to cover vacancy, ensuring it's protected against theft, fire, or damage.
- **When Needed**: Immediately upon securing the property, particularly if it will be vacant for an extended time.
- **Tip**: Vacant home insurance may be necessary, as standard homeowner policies often exclude vacant properties.

8. Utility Providers
- **Purpose**: Maintain essential services (electricity, heating, water) and prevent utility disruptions.

- **When Needed**: Upon securing the property, to maintain livable conditions and prevent deterioration.
- **Tip**: Contact each provider to notify them of the homeowner's passing and arrange continued service billing through the estate.

9. Appraiser
- **Purpose**: Provide an accurate valuation of the property and its contents for the probate inventory and eventual sale.
- **When Needed**: Soon after the property is secured, especially if there are high-value items or market-value clarity is needed.
- **Tip**: Hire an appraiser with expertise in probate and estate valuations to ensure accurate and court-compliant assessments.

10. Professional Home Inspector
- **Purpose**: Assess the property's condition, identify urgent repairs, and provide documentation for potential buyers or the probate court.
- **When Needed**: If the property requires extensive repairs or documentation of its condition.
- **Tip**: Inspectors can help prioritize maintenance tasks and prevent larger issues that could impact the property's value.

11. Maintenance and Repair Contractors
- **Purpose**: Handle immediate repairs (plumbing, electrical, roofing) and routine maintenance to maintain the property's value.
- **When Needed**: As soon as critical maintenance needs are identified, especially if safety is a concern.
- **Tip**: Work with trusted contractors familiar with estate properties, as their experience can help with the unique demands of vacant homes.

12. Tax Advisor or Accountant
- **Purpose**: Guide the executor on managing estate-related expenses, handling property taxes, and preparing for final tax filings.
- **When Needed**: Early in the process to set up accurate accounting and to handle property-related tax issues.

- **Tip**: A tax advisor experienced with estates can help optimize expenses related to the property and prepare the estate for eventual tax obligations.

Additional Tips

- **Document and Keep Receipts**: Record all expenses related to property security and maintenance, as these may be reimbursed by the estate or relevant to tax filings.

- **Rely on Professionals**: Probate properties often require unique care, and professionals bring both experience and efficiency, helping to reduce stress on family members.

- **Consult with a Probate Attorney Before Hiring**: Certain expenses may need court approval or careful documentation, and an attorney can guide the executor on which costs are appropriate.

This checklist ensures that every aspect of securing the property is covered by knowledgeable professionals, helping to protect both the property and the estate's value through the probate process.

Gathering Documentation

When a loved one passes, family members often find themselves tasked with sorting through paperwork and records as they work through the probate process. Although it may feel overwhelming, gathering the necessary documentation early on is crucial for an organized and efficient probate experience. This chapter provides a step-by-step guide to the key documents needed, where to locate them, and how to organize this information to prevent delays and complications in probate.

As always, this guide serves as an overview. Probate involves complex legal processes, and an experienced probate attorney is invaluable in helping you understand what documents are required and how to present them to the court.

Why Documentation Matters in Probate

In Illinois, the probate process is regulated by a series of rules and procedures designed to ensure that a decedent's assets are properly identified, valued, and transferred to heirs or creditors. This process requires documentation not only to verify the decedent's assets and debts but also to confirm legal authority to administer these assets. Failing to gather the right documents early can lead to delays, additional court filings, and in some cases, disputes among heirs.

Executors, or those responsible for managing the estate, are legally required to present accurate and complete information to the court. Illinois probate law mandates that executors submit an **inventory** listing the decedent's assets and debts within a certain timeframe, typically within 60 days of appointment. This means that collecting documentation quickly and accurately is essential to moving the probate process forward.

Key Documents to Gather

The Death Certificate

- **Purpose**: The death certificate is the foundational document for initiating probate. It serves as proof of the decedent's passing and is required by the court, financial institutions, and many other entities involved in the probate process.

- **Where to Obtain**: Death certificates are typically issued by the county health department where the death occurred. In Illinois, multiple copies can be ordered, and it is advisable to have several on hand, as most institutions require an original certified copy.

- **Tip**: Order extra copies (5–10) to accommodate various requests from banks, insurance companies, and government agencies, each of which often requires a certified original.

The Will (If One Exists)

- **Purpose**: If the decedent had a will, this document outlines their wishes regarding asset distribution and may appoint an executor. The will is crucial to probate because it informs the court of the decedent's intent for their assets.

- **Where to Find It**: Wills are often stored in safe deposit boxes, home safes, or with an attorney. Some individuals may also leave a copy with a trusted family member.

- **Submitting the Will**: In Illinois, the will must be submitted to the court within 30 days of the decedent's death. Failing to do so could complicate probate or potentially invalidate the will.

- **Tip**: Ensure you have the original document. A probate attorney can help determine the will's validity and provide guidance if multiple or conflicting wills are found.

Trust Documents (If Applicable)

- **Purpose**: If the decedent had a living trust, this document could include instructions for assets held outside of probate. Trusts can sometimes help bypass probate, but any assets outside the trust will still require probate proceedings.

- **Where to Find It**: Trust documents may be stored with the decedent's attorney or in a safe deposit box.

- **Tip**: It's beneficial to work with both a probate attorney and a trust attorney if there is a trust involved, as different professionals may specialize in these distinct areas of estate planning.

Deeds and Titles to Real Estate

- **Purpose**: Deeds and titles verify ownership of any real estate property owned by the decedent. These documents will help the executor confirm whether properties are subject to probate.

- **Where to Find Them**: Deeds may be stored with the decedent's personal records, in safe deposit boxes, or available at the county recorder's office. In Illinois, county recorders maintain copies of all real estate deeds, which can be obtained for a fee.

- **Tip**: Be sure to identify whether properties are solely owned, jointly owned, or held in trust, as this determines if they must go through probate.

Financial Statements

- **Purpose**: Financial statements help assess the decedent's assets, including bank accounts, retirement accounts, stocks, and bonds. Executors need accurate financial records to create the estate inventory and determine estate value.

- **Where to Find Them**: Look for recent statements for each account in the decedent's records or contact financial institutions directly. Digital accounts may require access to the decedent's email or online banking accounts.

- **Tip**: Many financial institutions require a death certificate and court authorization before providing account information, so having these on hand will streamline the process.

Insurance Policies

- **Purpose**: Life insurance policies, health insurance records, and homeowner's insurance policies are essential documents for both asset valuation and protection. Life insurance policies can provide financial support to the estate or designated beneficiaries.

- **Where to Find Them**: Policies may be stored at home, in a safe deposit box, or with the insurance company. Many companies provide policy information online, accessible with account credentials.

- **Tip**: Verify if any insurance benefits are payable directly to named beneficiaries, as these may be non-probate assets and not included in the probate inventory.

Tax Returns

- **Purpose**: Previous years' tax returns provide valuable insight into the decedent's income, assets, and possible deductions. Tax returns are necessary for completing the estate's final tax filings and for identifying potential assets not listed elsewhere.

- **Where to Find Them**: Look for copies in the decedent's personal records or with their accountant. The IRS can also provide past tax returns if necessary.

- **Tip**: A tax advisor or accountant familiar with estate taxes can be invaluable, as they can help ensure accurate and timely filing of the decedent's final tax return and any required estate tax returns.

Debts and Liabilities

- **Purpose**: Part of the executor's role is to pay off outstanding debts from the estate, so a full understanding of liabilities is critical. Common debts include mortgages, credit cards, personal loans, and medical bills.

- **Where to Find Them**: Review recent bills or statements, and consider contacting creditors directly. The decedent's mail or online accounts can also be a source of updated billing information.

- **Tip**: Illinois probate law requires that creditors be notified of the decedent's passing, and executors should pay debts in a specific order. A probate attorney can assist with this priority list to prevent liability issues.

Organizing and Managing Probate Documentation

Create a Filing System

Managing probate documents is far easier with a structured filing system. Consider creating a physical or digital filing system, with categories for each type of document (e.g., assets, debts, legal documents, etc.). Organizing documents upfront can prevent confusion or misplacement, saving time and stress down the road.

Keep Copies and Originals Separate

Some probate proceedings require original documents, while others accept copies. Always separate originals from copies to avoid unnecessary wear and tear on crucial papers like the death certificate, will, and deeds. Digital copies of all documents can also serve as a backup, which may be beneficial if you are working with out-of-state professionals.

Track Expenses and Communications

As the executor, you may incur expenses while gathering documents or meeting legal requirements. It's essential to document every cost and keep receipts, as these expenses may be reimbursed from the estate. Additionally, track all communications with professionals and institutions, noting dates and outcomes, to create a record for future reference.

Consult with Professionals

Gathering documentation can be complex, particularly when legal, financial, or tax records are involved. Probate attorneys, accountants, and real estate professionals who specialize in estates can guide you in gathering and organizing these records. If there is any doubt about whether a document is needed, consulting with a probate attorney early can prevent unnecessary delays or the need to backtrack.

Final Note: The Importance of Professional Help

The process of gathering documentation for probate can be time-consuming and requires a meticulous approach. By consulting with a probate attorney or estate professional early in this process, families can feel confident that they are fully prepared for the legal and financial obligations of probate. Additionally, a qualified professional can help identify less-obvious documents, such as business interests or personal property records, that may be essential for a comprehensive estate inventory.

This "Who, not how" approach ensures that the family has the right support, avoiding the pitfalls of trying to handle complex probate documentation independently. Probate attorneys, tax advisors, and experienced real estate professionals provide the legal and financial insight needed to navigate this initial step successfully, saving families time and offering peace of mind.

Identifying the Executor or Administrator

In Illinois, the person who is legally responsible for managing a deceased individual's estate is known as an executor (if appointed by the will) or an administrator (if appointed by the court when no will exists or when no executor is named). This individual plays a crucial role in the probate process, managing the estate's assets, paying debts, and ultimately distributing the inheritance according to the decedent's wishes or state laws. Identifying and appointing the executor or administrator early on is essential, as this role comes with significant legal obligations and responsibilities.

This chapter outlines the differences between executors and administrators, explains how each is appointed, and highlights the key responsibilities they hold in the Illinois probate process. Remember, this guide provides an overview, and a probate attorney is indispensable in helping families navigate the complexities of selecting and supporting the estate's representative.

Understanding the Role of an Executor or Administrator

The executor or administrator is the central figure in the probate process, acting as the estate's representative under the supervision of the court. This role is both an honor and a responsibility, as the chosen individual has a legal obligation to carry out duties in the best interest of the estate and its beneficiaries. Illinois law grants this person a "fiduciary duty," meaning they must act with the utmost honesty and integrity when handling estate matters.

While the specific tasks may vary depending on the size and complexity of the estate, the core responsibilities of an executor or administrator include:

> **Inventorying Assets:** Compiling a complete list of all estate assets, including real estate, bank accounts, personal property, and investments.

Paying Debts and Taxes: Identifying and paying any outstanding debts, taxes, and expenses associated with the estate.

Distributing Assets: Ensuring that beneficiaries receive their inheritance according to the will or, if no will exists, according to Illinois intestacy laws.

Maintaining Estate Records: Keeping detailed records of all transactions, communications, and distributions related to the estate.

These responsibilities come with strict requirements set by the Illinois Probate Act, and failure to perform them diligently can lead to legal repercussions for the executor or administrator.

How Executors are Appointed in Illinois

Appointment by the Will

If the decedent created a will, they likely named an executor within it. This person is typically a trusted family member, close friend, or a professional such as an attorney. The court generally honors the decedent's choice unless there is a compelling reason not to (e.g., if the named executor is unwilling, deceased, or legally unfit to serve).

To formally assume their role, the named executor must:

File a petition for probate with the court in the county where the decedent resided. This initiates the probate process and requests the court's recognition of the will and the executor's appointment.

Submit a certified copy of the death certificate and the original will. The court may require the executor to provide additional documents verifying their eligibility, especially if the will was contested or unclear.

Attend a court hearing, during which the judge reviews the will, appoints the executor, and issues letters of office (also known as letters testamentary). These letters officially authorize the executor to manage the estate and handle assets.

Appointment When No Will Exists (Intestate Estates)

If no will exists, the decedent's estate is considered intestate, meaning it will be distributed according to Illinois state laws rather than the decedent's wishes. In such cases, the court will appoint an administrator instead of an executor. Family members, typically a surviving spouse or adult child, may petition the court to be appointed as the administrator, or the court may assign an impartial administrator if family members cannot agree on a representative.

To be appointed as an administrator:

The interested party files a petition for letters of administration in the probate court. This petition requests permission to administer the estate, demonstrating the petitioner's relationship to the decedent and willingness to take on the role.

The court schedules a hearing to review the petition and determine eligibility. Illinois probate courts require administrators to meet specific legal criteria, such as being over the age of 18 and not having certain criminal convictions.

Once approved, the court grants letters of administration, which authorize the administrator to perform their duties. In some cases, administrators may need to post a surety bond (a form of insurance) to protect the estate in case of mismanagement.

Eligibility and Qualifications for Executors and Administrators

Illinois probate law sets specific eligibility requirements for executors and administrators, primarily to ensure that the appointed person is capable of handling the estate's complex financial and legal responsibilities.

General Requirements

Age: The executor or administrator must be at least 18 years old.

Residency: While Illinois does not require executors to be residents of Illinois, non-resident executors may need to designate a local agent or attorney to accept legal documents on their behalf.

Mental Competency: The person must be mentally competent to carry out fiduciary duties, as the role involves handling sensitive legal and financial matters.

Criminal Background: Individuals with certain felony convictions may be disqualified, especially those involving financial misconduct or fraud, as they could present a risk to the estate's assets.

Factors to Consider in Choosing an Executor or Administrator

For those selecting an executor or administrator (or if multiple family members are petitioning for the role), several factors should be taken into account:

Ability to Handle Complex Financial Tasks: Executors manage substantial financial responsibilities, including filing tax returns and handling distributions.

Communication Skills: Executors and administrators often mediate among beneficiaries and creditors, so they should be able to communicate clearly and diplomatically.

Time and Availability: Serving as an executor can be time-consuming, so the person chosen should have the availability to manage estate matters over several months or even years.

Objectivity and Fairness: Executors often navigate family dynamics, and someone perceived as neutral and fair can help prevent disputes among heirs.

Selecting a probate attorney can help resolve questions around who should serve as executor or administrator, as they can advise on eligibility, the appointment process, and the unique challenges of the role.

Executor or Administrator Responsibilities and Duties

Once appointed, the executor or administrator assumes a range of duties. While these can vary depending on the estate's complexity, Illinois probate law generally requires the following steps:

Inventorying Assets and Debts

The executor must compile an inventory of all assets and debts, including real estate, bank accounts, personal property, and outstanding loans. This document must be filed with the court within 60 days of the executor's appointment and provides transparency for all beneficiaries and creditors involved.

Managing and Protecting Assets

Executors and administrators are responsible for maintaining and securing estate assets. This may involve tasks such as:

Ensuring property remains insured and secured.

Paying ongoing bills like utilities, property taxes, and mortgage payments.

Arranging for necessary repairs or maintenance to protect the property's value.

Paying Debts and Taxes

One of the executor's primary responsibilities is to identify and pay off estate debts, including medical bills, credit cards, and any outstanding loans. Additionally, the executor must handle final income tax filings for the decedent and, if applicable, estate taxes.

Distributing Assets to Beneficiaries

Once all debts and expenses have been settled, the executor or administrator distributes remaining assets to the beneficiaries according to the will or state law. This process must be documented and approved by the court, particularly if minor or incapacitated beneficiaries are involved.

Maintaining Detailed Records

Executors and administrators must keep meticulous records of all transactions, expenses, and distributions related to the estate. Illinois probate courts may request these records to verify proper estate management, and clear documentation can prevent disputes with beneficiaries.

When to Seek Professional Assistance

Serving as an executor or administrator is a demanding role that often benefits from professional guidance. Probate attorneys are crucial allies, helping the estate representative understand legal obligations and deadlines, particularly when resolving disputes, managing complex assets, or navigating tax obligations.

Consulting with a Probate Attorney

A probate attorney can advise on the initial steps, guide the executor through Illinois probate procedures, and provide legal representation in court if needed. They ensure compliance with Illinois Probate Act requirements, prevent errors, and help resolve conflicts with creditors or beneficiaries.

Working with a Probate-Experienced Real Estate Agent

If real estate is part of the estate, a real estate agent specializing in probate can provide market analysis, help secure the property, and handle the sale in accordance with court requirements. They offer valuable insight into maintaining the property's value and managing market conditions during the probate period.

Engaging an Accountant or Tax Advisor

Executors and administrators may find it helpful to work with a tax advisor who specializes in estate taxes. This professional can help the representative navigate Illinois tax laws, manage final tax returns, and avoid potential penalties.

Final Note: Understanding the Weight of the Role

Identifying and appointing the right executor or administrator is critical to the probate process. This role requires an individual who can manage financial, legal, and interpersonal responsibilities, often while balancing family dynamics. By consulting with professionals early and often, executors and administrators can confidently fulfill their duties and protect the estate for its beneficiaries.

Adopting the "Who, not how" approach—leveraging the expertise of professionals in probate law, real estate, and taxes—can significantly ease the burden on executors and administrators, providing them with the knowledge and support to carry out their role effectively and lawfully.

The Executor's Role in Real Estate

Real estate is often one of the most significant and valuable assets in an estate, making its management a critical responsibility for the executor or administrator. In Illinois, probate law outlines specific steps and considerations for executors tasked with managing real estate through probate. This chapter provides an in-depth look at these duties, from securing the property to preparing it for sale or distribution, while reinforcing the importance of professional guidance in navigating these complex tasks.

Executors are strongly encouraged to consult a probate attorney and a real estate professional experienced in probate to ensure they are meeting legal requirements and making informed decisions that benefit the estate and its beneficiaries.

Securing and Maintaining Real Estate Assets

One of the executor's first real estate-related duties is securing any property owned by the decedent to protect its value and condition. As outlined in Section 2.1, securing the property includes tasks such as changing locks, setting up security systems, and notifying local authorities of the property's vacant status. However, the executor's responsibilities go beyond immediate security measures and extend to long-term maintenance.

Ensuring Continued Insurance Coverage

Maintaining homeowners' insurance coverage is essential. Many standard insurance policies do not cover vacant properties, which leaves them vulnerable to uncovered damages if incidents like fire, theft, or vandalism occur. Executors should notify the insurance provider of the decedent's passing and the property's vacant status to update the policy accordingly. In some cases, vacant property insurance may be necessary to ensure full coverage.

Managing Utilities and Essential Services

Keeping utilities active—such as electricity, water, heating, and air conditioning—helps prevent property damage, particularly during Illinois' extreme seasonal temperatures. For example, in winter, a heated home prevents pipes from freezing and bursting. Executors should review and pay utility bills using estate funds and, if possible, arrange for automated payments to avoid service disruptions.

Routine Maintenance and Repairs

To preserve the property's value, executors should manage routine maintenance, including lawn care, pest control, and basic repairs. Neglecting maintenance can lead to issues that may reduce the property's value or make it harder to sell. An experienced property management company or real estate professional can assist with these tasks, particularly if the executor is located out of state or lacks time.

Property Inventory and Valuation

To comply with Illinois probate requirements, the executor must assess the property's value and document it in the estate's inventory, a report filed with the probate court. This valuation is critical because it affects the estate's overall value, impacts decisions about debts and taxes, and guides how the property is eventually distributed or sold.

Determining Market Value Through Appraisal

An appraisal conducted by a licensed real estate appraiser provides an objective market value for the property. Appraisers consider factors such as recent sales of comparable properties, the home's condition, and the neighborhood. In Illinois, probate courts generally require a formal appraisal to verify the property's value, as this affects inheritance taxes and distribution among heirs.

Comparative Market Analysis (CMA)

While an appraisal provides an official valuation, a **Comparative Market Analysis** (CMA), prepared by a probate-experienced real estate agent, can offer insight into what the property might sell for on the open market. CMAs compare the property to similar homes in the area that have recently sold, providing a realistic estimate of market conditions. This analysis can be helpful if the property will be listed for sale, as it allows the executor to set an appropriate asking price.

Recording Property-Specific Liabilities

In addition to valuing the property, the executor should review any outstanding liabilities tied to the real estate, such as mortgages, liens, or unpaid property taxes. Identifying these debts early helps prevent delays later and ensures that any encumbrances on the property are managed within probate proceedings.

Deciding Whether to Sell or Retain the Property

The executor's decision to sell or retain the property depends on the instructions in the will, the preferences of heirs, and the estate's financial needs. If the will specifies that the property should be distributed to specific beneficiaries, the executor must follow these wishes, provided there are sufficient funds to cover debts and expenses. However, if the will is silent on the property, the executor must consider various factors when deciding on a sale.

Reviewing the Decedent's Will or Trust Instructions

In some cases, the will may specify that a property be kept within the family or transferred directly to a specific beneficiary. If so, the executor should work with a probate attorney to follow these instructions, ensuring compliance with Illinois probate law and confirming that beneficiaries agree with the planned distribution.

Selling to Cover Debts and Expenses

In Illinois, executors are required to use estate assets to pay off outstanding debts before distributing inheritances. If the estate lacks sufficient liquid assets (e.g., cash, stocks) to cover debts, the executor may need to sell the property. A probate attorney can provide guidance on obtaining court approval if necessary, as certain sales require court oversight, particularly if heirs contest the sale.

Balancing Family Dynamics and Preferences

Heirs often have strong emotional ties to family property, and disputes can arise if opinions differ on whether to keep or sell the home. An executor's role is to remain neutral and prioritize the best interests of the estate. Professional mediation or legal counsel can be helpful if there are conflicting views, ensuring that all family members feel heard and that the decision complies with Illinois probate laws.

Preparing the Property for Sale

If selling the property is the best course of action, the executor must prepare it for listing. Probate properties often require specific preparation to attract buyers, maintain market value, and meet legal standards. Working with a real estate agent experienced in probate sales can simplify this process and provide valuable guidance.

Making Necessary Repairs or Improvements

While probate properties are often sold "as-is," certain repairs may increase the home's value or make it more marketable. Minor fixes, such as fresh paint, cleaning, and basic landscaping, can enhance the property's appeal without significant investment. However, major renovations should be avoided unless they are essential to the sale, as probate properties are generally sold without extensive upgrades.

Complying with Disclosure Laws

In Illinois, sellers, including executors, are legally required to disclose known issues with the property, such as structural defects, water damage, or pest problems. Full disclosure protects the executor from potential legal issues and helps buyers make informed decisions. A real estate agent can assist with preparing these disclosures accurately and ensure compliance with Illinois real estate laws.

Coordinating Listing and Marketing with a Probate Real Estate Agent

A probate-experienced real estate agent understands the unique needs of probate properties and can manage the listing, marketing, and sale efficiently. They will advise on competitive pricing, target marketing, and negotiation strategies tailored to probate properties. This expertise ensures the property is positioned well in the market and that the executor has professional support throughout the sale.

Navigating the Sale Process and Court Approvals

Probate sales often require additional steps and, in some cases, court approvals, particularly if there are disputes among heirs or specific instructions in the will. Executors should prepare for a potentially different process than a standard home sale.

Accepting Offers and Court Confirmation

In Illinois, an executor may need court approval before finalizing the sale, especially if the property sale is contested or if it constitutes a large portion of the estate's value. The court will review the terms to ensure the sale aligns with the best interests of the estate and its beneficiaries. A probate attorney can advise on the court's specific requirements and represent the executor in court if needed.

Finalizing the Sale and Handling Proceeds

Once the property sale is approved, the executor oversees the closing process. Proceeds from the sale must be deposited into the estate account and used first to pay off any remaining debts or taxes. Any funds left over after all obligations are met can be distributed to heirs in accordance with the will or Illinois intestate succession laws.

A probate attorney and real estate professional can help manage these steps, ensuring compliance with legal requirements and reducing the risk of disputes among heirs regarding the sale proceeds.

Managing Challenges and Legal Considerations

Real estate in probate often involves unique challenges, from emotional attachments among heirs to legal complexities surrounding property distribution. Executors may face pressure from family members, financial constraints, or logistical difficulties. Working with knowledgeable professionals can help them address these challenges effectively.

Handling Disputes Among Heirs

It's common for family members to have conflicting preferences regarding the family home, particularly if it holds sentimental value. Executors can facilitate discussions, but they may also need to involve an attorney or mediator to resolve disputes fairly. Illinois probate courts are equipped to handle disputes, but avoiding litigation is generally preferable for all parties.

Complying with Illinois Probate Court Deadlines

The Illinois probate process includes specific timelines for actions like submitting an inventory, filing tax returns, and distributing assets. Executors who are unfamiliar with these deadlines risk penalties or delays in estate resolution. A probate attorney can help executors stay on track, meeting all required deadlines and avoiding potential complications.

Staying Neutral and Professional

An executor's role is to act in the estate's best interest, even if it means making difficult or unpopular decisions. By maintaining transparency, clear communication, and a neutral stance, executors can manage expectations and avoid unnecessary conflict. Professional guidance provides the executor with the tools to navigate these challenges objectively and confidently.

Final Note: The Value of Professional Assistance in Probate Real Estate

Executors are entrusted with the significant responsibility of managing real estate in probate, a task that requires diligence, neutrality, and attention to legal details. By seeking support from a probate attorney and a probate-experienced real estate agent, executors can ensure that each step—from securing and maintaining the property to navigating the sale process—is handled properly.

Following a "Who, not how" approach allows executors to focus on fulfilling their fiduciary duty while relying on the expertise of professionals who understand Illinois probate real estate. This collaborative approach not only streamlines the process but also provides peace of mind to the executor and family members alike, knowing that the property is in good hands.

Summary

Key Steps After a Loved One's Passing

Chapter 2 focuses on the immediate responsibilities facing executors and family members after a loved one's passing, highlighting the foundational steps needed to secure and prepare the estate for probate. Here are the primary takeaways:

1. **Securing the Property**: One of the first steps in managing the estate is securing the decedent's property to protect it from potential risks, such as theft, vandalism, or neglect. Executors should consider practical measures like changing locks, maintaining insurance coverage, and arranging for property upkeep to preserve the estate's value during probate.

2. **Gathering Essential Documentation**: Accurate records are crucial to a successful probate process. Executors should gather key documents, including the death certificate, will (if one exists), deeds, financial statements, and insurance policies. This documentation will support estate inventory, court filings, and other essential probate requirements.

3. **Identifying the Executor or Administrator**: The probate process requires an official representative to manage the estate. If there is a will, the court typically appoints the executor named within it. In cases where no will exists, an administrator will be appointed by the court, usually a close relative. This individual has legal responsibilities to protect and manage the estate according to Illinois law.

4. **Understanding the Executor's Role in Real Estate**: Executors have specific duties related to managing any real estate in the estate, from securing and maintaining the property to deciding whether to sell or retain it. They are responsible for ensuring the property remains in good condition, managing any debts or liens, and preparing it for sale if necessary. Working with real estate and legal professionals can be especially helpful in carrying out these duties effectively.

Chapter 2 emphasizes the importance of early action, careful organization, and professional support. By securing the property, gathering vital documents, and understanding their responsibilities, executors are well-prepared to initiate probate and manage the estate efficiently on behalf of all beneficiaries.

Checklist: Key Initial Steps After a Loved One's Passing

1. Securing the Property
- ☐ Change locks and ensure all entry points are secure to prevent unauthorized access to the property.
- ☐ Confirm that utilities (electricity, heat, water) are operational if needed to protect the property from weather-related damage.
- ☐ Consider setting up a security system or notifying local law enforcement that the property is temporarily vacant.
- ☐ Notify neighbors about the property's vacancy status, if applicable, so they can report any suspicious activity.

2. Gathering Essential Documentation
- ☐ Locate and collect key documents, such as:
    - ☐ Titles and deeds for real estate properties.
    - ☐ The decedent's will and any trusts or estate planning documents.
    - ☐ Financial statements, including bank accounts, retirement accounts, investment portfolios, and outstanding debts.
    - ☐ Life insurance policies and beneficiary designations.
    - ☐ Tax returns, as they may provide insight into assets, liabilities, and income sources.
- ☐ Create a secure file or digital record for all documentation to streamline the probate process.

3. Identifying the Executor or Administrator
- ☐ Determine if a will exists that designates an executor. If so, confirm their willingness and eligibility to serve in this role.
    - ☐ If no will exists, check Illinois probate rules to see who may be eligible to serve as an administrator, as the court may appoint someone based on state priority guidelines.
- ☐ Understand that the executor or administrator will be responsible for managing the estate, including real estate, financial matters, and probate documentation.

4. Understanding the Executor's Role in Real Estate
- ☐ Inventory the real estate and assess any immediate maintenance needs, repairs, or security issues.

☐ Arrange for an initial property valuation to understand its approximate market value, which can help with decisions regarding sale or transfer.

☐ Notify heirs and beneficiaries about the property status and explain any planned steps for managing or preparing the property.

☐ Begin reviewing property expenses (mortgage, property taxes, insurance, and maintenance costs) to ensure they are managed responsibly during probate.

Chapter 3

Opening Probate in Illinois Courts

Opening probate is the formal process of petitioning the court to oversee the estate's administration. In Illinois, this begins with filing specific paperwork, attending initial court proceedings, and meeting certain legal requirements to appoint an executor or administrator. This chapter walks you through each step of filing a petition, preparing for court, and understanding the associated fees. Knowing what to expect in these early proceedings is crucial, as it sets the stage for managing the estate's assets, debts, and real estate holdings throughout the probate process.

Filing a Petition for Probate

Starting the probate process requires filing a petition with the court to formally request the court's oversight in managing and distributing the decedent's assets. For families facing this process in Illinois, understanding the steps, required documents, and legal requirements can help ensure a smooth initiation of probate. Filing a petition is the first formal step and establishes the court's authority over the estate while confirming who will manage it, either as executor or administrator.

This section covers the essentials of filing a petition for probate, including the documents you need, filing fees, and why working with a probate attorney is often beneficial at this stage.

What is a Petition for Probate?

A petition for probate is a formal request to the probate court asking it to recognize the decedent's will (if there is one), confirm the appointment of an executor, or appoint an administrator if no will exists. This petition effectively initiates the probate process, giving the court the legal authority to oversee asset distribution and debt payment, all in accordance with Illinois law.

The petition for probate outlines key details about the decedent, their assets, and their intended beneficiaries or heirs. The court relies on this petition to appoint a representative—either the person named in the will (executor) or someone chosen by the court if no will exists (administrator)—to handle all estate matters in line with Illinois Probate Act requirements.

Steps to Filing a Petition for Probate in Illinois

Filing a petition for probate involves several specific steps, and understanding each can help the executor or administrator prepare effectively.

Prepare the Petition for Probate

The first step is to complete the official **Petition for Probate** form, available through the Illinois probate court system or, in many cases, on the website of the circuit court where the petition will be filed. The form requires essential details about the decedent, such as:

- **The Decedent's Information**: Full name, date of death, last known address, and Social Security number.

- **The Decedent's Family**: List of surviving family members and heirs, including spouses, children, and other potential beneficiaries.

- **Will or No Will (Intestate)**: Confirmation of whether the decedent left a valid will or died intestate (without a will).

- **Executor or Administrator Request**: If the decedent left a will, the petitioner requests that the court formally appoint the executor named in it. If there is no will, the petitioner requests to be appointed as administrator or nominate another qualified individual.

It's advisable to work with a probate attorney at this stage to ensure the petition is completed accurately. Incomplete or incorrect information can delay the probate process, resulting in additional court fees and time-consuming corrections.

Gather Required Documents

To complete the filing, several essential documents must accompany the petition. These documents confirm the decedent's passing, validate the will, and provide the court with a full understanding of the estate.

- **Death Certificate**: A certified copy of the death certificate is necessary to confirm the date of death. Most probate courts require an official, certified copy, which can be obtained from the Illinois Department of Public Health or the county health department.

- **Original Will (if Applicable)**: If the decedent left a will, the original document must be presented to the court, along with any codicils (amendments to the will). Illinois law requires that the will be filed with the court within 30 days of the decedent's death.

- **Supporting Affidavits**: If the will includes witnesses, the court may require affidavits from those witnesses confirming the will's validity. Often, these affidavits are included in the will itself. If not, a probate attorney can assist in obtaining witness affidavits to avoid delays.

Pay the Filing Fee

Filing fees vary by county in Illinois but generally range from $300 to $500, depending on the jurisdiction. These fees cover court costs associated with processing the petition and managing the probate case. Executors or administrators should be prepared to pay this fee upfront, as it is required to officially open probate. The fee can typically be reimbursed from estate funds once probate has been established.

Submit the Petition and Attend the Initial Hearing

Once all forms and documents are complete, the petition can be filed in the circuit court of the county where the decedent resided. After submitting the petition, the court schedules an initial hearing, where a judge will review the submitted documents, verify the validity of the will (if applicable), and confirm the appointment of the executor or administrator.

At the hearing, the court will:

- Verify that the will is legally valid and signed by the decedent and witnesses.

- Appoint the executor named in the will or, in the absence of a will, appoint an administrator.

- Issue **letters of office** (also known as **letters testamentary** for executors and **letters of administration** for administrators), which serve as legal documentation that the appointed representative has authority to act on behalf of the estate.

Executors and administrators often benefit from attending this hearing with a probate attorney, who can address questions from the court, clarify any complexities, and ensure that the proceedings move forward smoothly.

Appointing an Executor or Administrator

When a decedent has left a will, the court typically honors their choice of executor, appointing the person named in the will unless there is a compelling reason not to (such as if the executor declines the role, is deceased, or is legally disqualified). However, when no will exists, the court appoints an administrator from among the closest relatives, usually a spouse, adult child, or another heir.

Qualifications for Executors and Administrators

In Illinois, the appointed executor or administrator must meet certain requirements:

- **Age**: The representative must be at least 18 years old.

- **Mental Competency**: They must be mentally capable of handling the estate's responsibilities.

- **No Disqualifying Criminal History**: Individuals with felony convictions, particularly those related to financial misconduct, may be disqualified.

- **Residency Considerations**: Non-resident executors may need to appoint a local agent or work with an attorney to meet Illinois requirements for accepting legal documents on their behalf.

Bond Requirements for Administrators

When no will exists or when the will does not specifically waive bond, Illinois probate law may require administrators to post a **surety bond**. A bond is a form of insurance that protects the estate from potential mismanagement by the administrator. The court sets the bond amount based on the value of the estate, and the administrator may purchase this bond through a bonding company.

Responsibilities Following the Appointment

Once appointed, the executor or administrator has fiduciary duties to the estate and its beneficiaries, which include managing assets, paying debts, and distributing inheritance according to the will or Illinois intestate laws. Their first responsibilities include the following:

Notifying Heirs and Creditors

The appointed executor or administrator is responsible for notifying heirs, beneficiaries, and creditors of the probate proceedings. Illinois probate law requires that all known heirs be notified of the hearing, and creditors must receive a notice of the decedent's death to allow them the opportunity to make claims against the estate. This step is critical to ensure transparency and prevent disputes later in the probate process.

Inventorying Estate Assets

Within 60 days of appointment, the executor must file an inventory of all known assets with the court. This inventory lists real estate, bank accounts, personal property, stocks, bonds, and other assets in the decedent's name. Compiling this inventory accurately is essential to meeting Illinois probate requirements and ensuring fair distribution to beneficiaries.

When to Seek Professional Assistance

Filing a petition for probate is a legal process with specific requirements that, if overlooked, can delay the probate process or even result in legal disputes. Working with a probate attorney from the outset provides invaluable support and helps ensure each step is handled correctly.

Engaging a Probate Attorney

A probate attorney can assist in completing the petition accurately, gathering the necessary documentation, and attending the initial court hearing. They can also clarify any specific legal requirements based on the county where the petition is filed, as certain rules and procedures may vary by jurisdiction. Legal guidance at this stage is especially important if there is any question about the will's validity or if family members anticipate disagreements over estate management.

Consulting a Tax Advisor or Accountant

In some cases, it is helpful to work with an accountant or tax advisor familiar with estate taxation to ensure that the decedent's financial records are organized, particularly if there are complex assets or tax considerations. They can assist the executor or administrator in setting up proper estate accounting practices from the outset, which can simplify asset inventorying and tax filing later in the probate process.

Final Note: Practical Considerations for Filing the Petition for Probate

Filing a petition for probate is a detailed process that establishes the foundation for managing the estate effectively. Accuracy, timely filing, and thorough preparation are essential to keeping the probate process on track. Executors and administrators should pay close attention to required documents, fees, and the details provided in the petition to avoid delays or errors that could complicate probate proceedings.

By being proactive in gathering the necessary information and seeking assistance when needed, family members or appointed representatives can ensure the probate process starts off smoothly, setting the stage for organized and fair estate administration. As the petition is filed and court proceedings begin, the executor or administrator will be equipped to move forward confidently with their duties, keeping the estate's best interests at the forefront.

Court Proceedings

Once the initial petition has been filed, Illinois probate law requires a formal court hearing to initiate the probate process officially. While some estates may require only minimal court interaction after this first hearing, others might involve additional court supervision or hearings, especially when assets are contested or legal complexities arise. This section will explain what the executor or administrator can expect during the initial court proceedings and outline scenarios that may require ongoing court involvement throughout probate.

The Purpose and Scope of the Initial Probate Hearing

The primary function of the initial probate hearing is to validate the will (if present), establish the executor's or administrator's authority, and ensure that all key parties are aware of the probate proceedings. This hearing is typically brief but serves as the probate court's way to set the stage for orderly estate administration under court supervision.

During this hearing:

- **Confirmation of Appointment**: The court formally appoints the executor or administrator, issuing them letters of office to act on behalf of the estate.

- **Legal Oversight**: The judge may review the estate's unique needs and determine whether additional oversight or hearings will be required.

- **Review of Estate Complexity**: The judge considers factors such as family disputes, creditor claims, and real estate or business interests that may warrant future court intervention.

The outcome of this hearing largely determines the level of court involvement required. Estates that are straightforward and uncontested may need little further court oversight, while those with contested assets or complex debts may see a more hands-on approach from the judge.

Preparing for Potential Challenges During Probate

While many initial probate hearings are procedural, certain situations may lead to further court proceedings, especially if the estate involves disputes or significant financial complexities.

Dealing with Will Contests and Heir Disputes

Contesting a will or disputing the executor's appointment can escalate probate proceedings. If an heir or interested party raises objections, the court may set a separate hearing to examine these claims in greater detail. For example:

- **Will Contests**: Grounds for contesting a will often include claims of undue influence, mental incapacity, or improper execution. The judge may request further documentation, such as affidavits from witnesses or medical records, to assess the validity of these claims.

- **Executor Challenges**: Family members may dispute the appointment of an executor, especially if they believe the individual is unfit. The judge may evaluate the concerns and decide whether a different executor should be appointed.

Probate attorneys play a crucial role in managing these conflicts. Executors should consider working with an attorney if they anticipate or encounter disputes, as legal guidance helps navigate these sensitive situations effectively.

Creditor Claims and Debt Resolution

During probate, creditors have the right to make claims against the estate for any unpaid debts. The court plays a supervisory role in ensuring these claims are legitimate and that the estate assets are used appropriately to satisfy debts.

Illinois requires executors to notify creditors early in probate. This notification period allows creditors to file claims, which the executor reviews and either accepts or disputes based on available estate funds. If multiple significant claims exist, the judge may hold additional hearings to approve the executor's proposed debt repayment plan. These proceedings help prevent creditors from taking legal action against the estate by providing a structured approach to debt resolution.

Handling Complex Assets or Real Estate

Some estates include assets that are not easily liquidated, such as businesses, valuable collections, or real estate. Managing these assets may require the court's ongoing oversight, particularly if:

- **Property is Disputed**: Real estate that multiple heirs wish to keep or sell often requires court approval to finalize decisions.

- **Businesses or Investments Need Valuation**: If the estate includes business holdings or complex investments, the court may request professional valuations to determine fair market value, especially if these assets are being divided among beneficiaries.

In these cases, the judge may order periodic check-ins to monitor the executor's progress with asset management and ensure actions align with Illinois probate requirements.

Working with the Court Throughout Probate

While some estates only require the initial court hearing, others may involve additional court interactions. Executors should be prepared to appear in court or submit reports if the judge requests updates, especially if the estate involves significant disputes or complex financial transactions. Common reasons for additional court oversight include:

Interim Accountings and Status Reports

For estates that are extensive or involve many creditors, the court may require the executor to submit interim accountings or status reports. These reports outline the estate's financial status, including asset management, debts paid, and any distributions made to beneficiaries. This level of oversight ensures transparency, particularly when multiple parties have a vested interest in the estate's progress.

Dispute Resolution Hearings

If disputes arise among heirs, creditors, or other interested parties, the court may schedule dispute resolution hearings. These hearings serve as structured opportunities to address disagreements and find mutually acceptable solutions. The judge may provide mediation options or guidance on reaching settlements that respect the estate's interests while satisfying all parties involved.

Final Distribution Hearing

Once all debts are paid and assets prepared for distribution, the court may schedule a final distribution hearing. During this hearing, the judge reviews the executor's actions, verifies that all estate obligations have been met, and authorizes the final transfer of remaining assets to beneficiaries. This hearing officially closes the probate case, providing closure for both the executor and heirs.

Practical Considerations for Executors in Court Proceedings

Navigating court proceedings can seem daunting, but a few practical tips can help executors manage these steps confidently:

Staying Organized

Court proceedings, especially for complex estates, often involve substantial documentation and regular updates. Executors should maintain organized records of all transactions, communications with beneficiaries and creditors, and any documents filed with the court. This organization makes it easier to provide clear and accurate reports when the court requests updates.

Communicating with Heirs and Beneficiaries

Executors are responsible for keeping beneficiaries informed of major court decisions, including approvals for asset sales or debt payments that affect their inheritance. Clear, proactive communication helps prevent misunderstandings or disputes, as heirs are less likely to challenge the executor's actions if they are well-informed throughout probate.

Seeking Professional Assistance

For executors handling complex estates or facing challenges in court, working with a probate attorney provides critical support. Attorneys can help manage court requirements, advise on legal strategies, and represent the executor in hearings. For cases involving taxes, complex assets, or substantial debts, consulting an accountant or tax professional can also ensure compliance with Illinois law and prevent costly errors.

Final Note: Embracing the Court's Role as a Support System

The court proceedings in probate exist not only to regulate the estate's management but also to offer support and resolution for executors, administrators, and beneficiaries. By working in cooperation with the court and following procedural requirements closely, executors can navigate probate with confidence, ensuring that the estate's assets are managed and distributed fairly and lawfully. Executors should view the probate court as an ally, especially in complex cases, and can rely on legal and financial professionals for guidance when court interactions become challenging.

Dealing with Illinois Probate Costs and Fees

Probate can involve a variety of costs, some of which may come as a surprise to families going through the process for the first time. Understanding the types of fees associated with probate in Illinois—and how to prepare for and manage them—can help the executor or administrator ensure that the estate is financially equipped to handle these expenses. This section offers a breakdown of typical probate costs, explains how fees are covered, and provides tips for budgeting throughout probate.

It's important to remember that while many probate expenses are necessary, executors have options for managing costs efficiently and may be able to recover expenses from estate funds.

Types of Probate Costs and Fees in Illinois

The costs of probate vary based on the estate's size, complexity, and any unique assets or liabilities involved. Here are the most common probate expenses to anticipate:

Court Filing Fees

Court filing fees are required to open probate and cover the administrative costs associated with processing the estate. In Illinois, these fees vary by county but generally range between $300 and $500 for the initial filing. Additional fees may be incurred if further petitions or motions are required during probate, especially if the estate is contested or involves complex assets.

Attorney Fees

Probate attorney fees can vary widely, depending on the estate's complexity and the amount of legal assistance required. In Illinois, probate attorneys typically charge either a flat fee, hourly rate, or a percentage of the estate's value. For straightforward estates, a flat fee may be negotiated, while more complex cases often require hourly billing, particularly if court appearances or dispute resolution are involved.

Illinois law does not set specific limits on attorney fees for probate cases, so it's crucial for the executor to clarify the fee structure in advance. In many cases, these fees can be paid from the estate, reducing the burden on the executor personally.

Executor or Administrator Fees

Illinois allows executors and administrators to receive fair compensation for their time and efforts in managing the estate. This fee can either be based on the complexity and workload involved or as a percentage of the estate's total value, depending on what the probate court deems reasonable.

While family members serving as executors may choose to waive this fee, especially in smaller estates, compensation is often warranted when the responsibilities are extensive. It's worth noting that any fees the executor receives are considered taxable income, so consulting a tax professional may be beneficial.

Appraisal Fees

Appraisals are often required to determine the fair market value of real estate, valuable personal property, or business interests included in the estate. Licensed appraisers charge a fee for this service, which varies based on the property's type and complexity. For Illinois real estate, appraisal fees typically range from $300 to $600, while appraisals for high-value assets like jewelry, collectibles, or artwork may cost more.

These appraisals are important for accurately reporting the estate's value to the court, as well as for tax purposes and equitable distribution among heirs.

Bond Fees

If the executor or administrator is required to post a bond—an insurance policy that protects the estate from potential mismanagement—there will be a bond premium based on the estate's size. The court may waive this requirement if the will specifies it, but when a bond is required, costs are typically 0.5% to 1% of the estate's total value annually.

The bond premium is often reimbursable from the estate's funds, and executors can seek guidance from the probate court or a bonding company to secure appropriate coverage.

Miscellaneous Fees

Additional costs in probate may include:

- **Accounting Fees**: For estates with complex financial holdings, executors may need professional accounting services to ensure accurate inventorying and reporting of assets.

- **Publication Fees**: Illinois law requires public notice of probate to inform creditors of the estate's opening. Publication costs vary but are generally minimal.

- **Property Maintenance Fees**: For real estate or other physical assets, costs may be incurred to maintain and secure the property during probate.

How Probate Costs Are Covered

One of the executor's key responsibilities is managing these costs in a way that preserves the estate's value. Fortunately, probate costs are generally paid from the estate's assets, not from the executor's personal funds. Here's a look at how these expenses are handled:

Using Estate Assets

Illinois probate law allows executors to use estate funds to cover probate-related expenses, meaning costs like court fees, appraisals, attorney fees, and executor compensation can be paid from the estate's cash accounts. When liquid assets (e.g., bank accounts) are limited, the executor may need to liquidate certain estate assets, such as investments or personal property, to cover these costs.

It's essential to document all probate expenses and keep clear records of payments, as the executor must provide an accounting of all costs to the probate court and beneficiaries. Working with an accountant or probate attorney can help ensure these expenses are properly tracked.

Managing Cash Flow

Some estates may lack immediate cash to pay upfront expenses, particularly if the decedent's assets are primarily tied up in real estate or investments. In such cases, executors may consider:

- **Short-Term Estate Loans**: Certain financial institutions and probate-specific lenders offer short-term loans to cover probate costs, allowing the executor to access funds that can later be repaid from estate assets once liquidated.

- **Partial Distributions**: In cases where only a portion of the estate assets are required for fees, executors may initiate limited distributions to cover costs while preserving other assets until probate is closed.

Reducing and Managing Probate Expenses

While some probate costs are unavoidable, there are strategies executors can use to minimize expenses and keep the estate's funds intact as much as possible.

Opting for "Independent Administration"

Illinois offers two primary types of probate administration: **independent administration** and **supervised administration**. Independent administration allows executors to manage the estate with minimal court involvement, which can reduce overall court fees, attorney costs, and administrative expenses. Independent administration is generally preferred in uncontested estates, as it offers a more streamlined process and fewer required court hearings.

Executors should consult a probate attorney to determine whether independent administration is suitable, as it's generally only available if all heirs agree and no significant disputes exist within the estate.

Negotiating Fees with Professionals

Attorneys, appraisers, and other professionals who serve estates often have flexible fee structures. Executors can sometimes negotiate a flat fee rather than an hourly rate for simpler cases, or request a payment plan for more complex cases that require significant legal or financial services. A probate attorney can also help evaluate which services are necessary and suggest areas where costs can be minimized.

Planning for Tax Deductibility

Some probate costs may be tax-deductible, particularly expenses related to managing and transferring real estate or investments. A tax advisor can help executors understand potential deductions available to the estate, reducing the overall tax burden. Proper tax planning can help the estate save on expenses during probate and leave more funds available for distribution to beneficiaries.

Preparing for Unexpected Probate Expenses

While executors can plan for certain known probate costs, unexpected expenses may arise, especially if disputes or unusual assets are involved. Here's how to prepare for potential surprises:

Setting a Realistic Budget

Creating a probate budget early in the process can help the executor manage estate funds efficiently. By estimating costs based on the estate's specific needs and setting aside funds for unanticipated expenses, the executor can avoid cash flow issues. For larger estates, a probate attorney or accountant can assist in creating a more detailed budget.

Reserving Funds for Potential Litigation

If there are known family disputes or complex assets in the estate, executors should prepare for potential legal fees associated with resolving these issues. Legal challenges can significantly increase probate costs, and having a contingency plan for attorney fees or court-related expenses is prudent when family dynamics are strained or heirs are likely to contest the will.

Communicating with Beneficiaries

Keeping beneficiaries informed about expected costs and the reasoning behind them can prevent misunderstandings and disputes. When beneficiaries understand the costs involved and the necessity of each expense, they are more likely to trust the executor's decisions and support cost-saving measures when appropriate.

Final Note: Managing Probate Costs Wisely

The costs associated with probate can add up, but executors have several tools and strategies for managing these expenses effectively. By understanding the types of fees involved, seeking professional guidance, and budgeting carefully, executors can navigate probate costs without compromising the estate's value or delaying distribution to heirs. Executors are encouraged to keep detailed records of all expenses and consult with financial professionals as needed to ensure that costs remain controlled and transparent to all parties involved in the probate process.

Summary

Chapter 3 guides executors through the foundational steps of initiating probate in Illinois, covering everything from filing the initial petition to understanding court requirements and handling probate-related expenses. Here are the essential points covered in this chapter:

1. **Filing a Petition for Probate**: The probate process begins with filing a formal petition in the Illinois probate court, which includes submitting necessary documents like the will (if one exists) and a certified death certificate. This step establishes the court's authority over the estate and formally appoints the executor or administrator, granting them legal responsibility to manage estate affairs.

2. **Navigating Court Proceedings**: Once the petition is filed, the initial court hearing confirms the executor or administrator's authority to act on behalf of the estate. This hearing also addresses any potential issues, such as will contests or disputes over the executor's appointment. The court's role throughout probate may vary based on the complexity of the estate, with additional hearings scheduled if there are disputes or complex assets involved.

3. **Understanding Probate Costs and Fees**: Probate can involve various costs, including court filing fees, attorney fees, appraisal costs, and executor compensation. Executors are responsible for managing these expenses from estate funds, ensuring that all fees are properly documented and paid before distributing assets to beneficiaries. Effective budgeting and, if necessary, working with professionals can help executors handle probate costs efficiently.

In summary, Chapter 3 emphasizes the importance of organized, proactive steps when opening probate. By filing the petition accurately, understanding the court's role, and budgeting for probate-related costs, executors are well-prepared to handle their duties within Illinois probate court requirements, ensuring a smoother process for both the estate and its beneficiaries.

Checklist: Key Steps for Opening Probate in Illinois Courts
1. Filing a Petition for Probate

    ☐ Gather necessary documents for the probate filing, including:

        ☐ The decedent's original will (if applicable).

        ☐ Death certificate.

        ☐ Relevant identification and contact information for heirs and beneficiaries.

        ☐ A preliminary list of the decedent's known assets and liabilities.

    ☐ Complete the appropriate probate forms, which can be obtained from the Illinois circuit court or probate division.

    ☐ File the petition for probate with the appropriate county court where the decedent resided or where their property is located.

    ☐ Pay the initial court filing fee, which may vary by county in Illinois.

2. Preparing for Court Proceedings

    ☐ Confirm the date for the initial probate hearing, which the court will schedule upon filing.

    ☐ Notify heirs, beneficiaries, and other interested parties of the probate hearing date, as required by Illinois law.

    ☐ Be prepared to present the will (if applicable) and validate its authenticity during the court hearing. If there is no will, be prepared to discuss the decedent's known heirs.

    ☐ Understand that the court will review all filed documents and may ask questions regarding the estate, its assets, and the proposed executor or administrator.

3. Appointing the Executor or Administrator

    ☐ Confirm that the person named in the will as executor is willing and able to serve in this role. If no executor is named or the person cannot serve, Illinois probate rules will help determine who may qualify as an administrator.

☐ Obtain *Letters of Office* (or *Letters Testamentary*), which the court will issue to the executor or administrator after appointment. These letters authorize the executor or administrator to act on behalf of the estate.

☐ Understand that the executor or administrator's responsibilities include inventorying assets, notifying creditors, and managing the estate's debts, taxes, and distributions.

4. Understanding Illinois Probate Costs and Fees

☐ Prepare for common probate-related expenses, including:

☐ Court filing fees and hearing costs.

☐ Appraisal fees for real estate or other significant assets.

☐ Bond fees (if required by the court), which serve as a safeguard to protect estate assets.

☐ Legal and accounting fees if professional assistance is needed for filing, asset valuation, or tax preparation.

☐ Document all fees and keep clear records, as the executor or administrator will need to report these expenses in the estate's final accounting.

Chapter 4

Valuing The Real Estate

Valuing real estate is a critical step in probate, as it determines the estate's overall worth and helps guide financial decisions moving forward. For executors in Illinois, it's essential to understand how the probate court assesses property value, when a formal appraisal is required, and how taxes may impact inherited real estate. This chapter provides an overview of appraisals, market analyses, and Illinois tax implications, equipping you with the knowledge needed to ensure the estate's assets are valued accurately and responsibly. By valuing the property correctly, you'll help protect the estate's financial integrity and support fair distribution among heirs.

Appraising the Property

In probate, accurately determining the value of real estate owned by the decedent is critical. An official appraisal is often necessary not only to meet court requirements but also to ensure fair distribution among heirs, determine tax obligations, and guide decisions about the future of the property. In Illinois, probate courts rely on these appraisals to verify the property's worth, so executors should approach the process with a clear understanding of the steps involved and the importance of professional valuation.

This section will outline the purpose of appraising property in probate, when an appraisal is necessary, how to select a qualified appraiser, and how the results of the appraisal impact other stages in the probate process.

The Purpose of Real Estate Appraisals in Probate

In probate, the executor's duty is to administer the estate accurately and fairly. Real estate is often one of the most valuable assets in an estate, and knowing its precise value has far-reaching implications. A real estate appraisal provides the probate court, creditors, and beneficiaries with an objective valuation of the property's fair market value as of the date of the decedent's passing. This valuation can impact key areas, such as:

- **Court Requirements**: Illinois probate courts often require an appraisal to ensure the estate inventory reflects true market values. This helps prevent disputes or challenges regarding asset worth and allows the court to monitor the estate's financial status accurately.

- **Distribution to Heirs**: In estates where the real estate is divided among multiple heirs or beneficiaries, an appraisal offers a fair basis for distribution, helping to prevent conflicts or claims of inequity.

- **Tax Obligations**: Illinois estate tax obligations and federal estate tax implications are based, in part, on the total value of the estate. A reliable real estate appraisal ensures accurate tax reporting and prevents underpayment or overpayment.

By establishing a property's appraised value, executors can meet their fiduciary duty to manage the estate responsibly, aligning decisions with Illinois probate laws and ensuring transparency with the court and beneficiaries.

When a Property Appraisal is Necessary

Not all probate cases in Illinois require a full appraisal of real estate, but certain conditions typically prompt the need for one:

Estates with Real Property Subject to Probate

For estates where real estate is titled solely in the decedent's name and, therefore, subject to probate, an appraisal is generally required. If the property is jointly owned or held in trust, it may transfer directly to beneficiaries without needing a formal probate appraisal. However, a probate attorney can provide guidance in unique cases or when unclear ownership structures exist.

Estates with Potential Tax Liabilities

If the estate's total value, including real estate and other assets, approaches or exceeds federal or Illinois estate tax thresholds, an accurate appraisal is essential. Even if tax thresholds are not met, the executor may still need an appraisal to complete required tax filings, especially if the decedent held other significant assets.

Properties Involved in Family Agreements or Sales

If the property is to be sold to a family member or if heirs wish to receive cash rather than an ownership interest, an appraisal establishes an objective sale price. This allows heirs to make informed decisions and prevents potential claims of favoritism or undervaluation. A clear, professional valuation is particularly helpful in keeping family agreements amicable and transparent.

Selecting a Qualified Real Estate Appraiser

An appraisal is only as reliable as the professional who conducts it. In Illinois, real estate appraisers must be licensed and certified, and executors should choose an appraiser experienced with probate properties, as they understand the unique requirements of estate valuation. Here are some considerations when selecting an appraiser:

Licensing and Certification Requirements

Appraisers in Illinois must hold a state license or certification. Executors can verify an appraiser's credentials through the Illinois Department of Financial and Professional Regulation, which maintains a registry of licensed appraisers. Working with a certified appraiser ensures that the valuation is reliable and that the appraiser meets Illinois' standards for real estate appraisal.

Experience with Probate and Estate Appraisals

Probate appraisals often have specific requirements that differ from standard property valuations. Executors should look for appraisers familiar with probate cases, as they understand court reporting requirements, IRS valuation standards, and the documentation needed to support probate filings. A probate-experienced appraiser can provide valuation formats that are tailored to court needs, simplifying the executor's task of filing the estate inventory.

Cost and Timing Considerations

Appraisal costs can vary depending on the property's location, type, and complexity. In Illinois, typical appraisal fees for residential properties range from $300 to $600, but properties with unique characteristics, like commercial properties or farms, may incur higher costs. It's advisable for executors to discuss both the fee structure and the timeline for completing the appraisal, as delays can affect court deadlines.

The Appraisal Process: What to Expect

The appraisal process is relatively straightforward but requires the executor's cooperation to provide the appraiser with access to the property and any pertinent details about its condition or recent updates. Here's what to expect:

Scheduling and Conducting the Appraisal

Once the appraiser is selected, they will schedule a site visit to the property. During the inspection, the appraiser assesses various aspects of the home, including its size, condition, layout, and any unique features. They will also evaluate the surrounding neighborhood, recent sales of comparable properties, and current market trends to arrive at a fair market value.

Reviewing the Appraisal Report

After the inspection, the appraiser compiles their findings into a formal appraisal report. This report includes the appraised value, a summary of the property's condition, and a detailed explanation of how the value was determined. The executor should review the report carefully and ensure they understand its contents, as it will be submitted to the court as part of the estate's official inventory.

Handling Appraisal Discrepancies or Adjustments

In some cases, appraisals may yield unexpected valuations, either higher or lower than anticipated. If heirs or interested parties dispute the value, the executor can consult a second appraiser or seek legal advice to clarify the results. However, it's important to remember that an appraisal reflects market conditions at the time of the decedent's passing, not necessarily a future sale price.

How the Appraised Value Impacts Probate Decisions

Once the appraisal is complete, the appraised value serves as a baseline for the court and guides several key decisions in the probate process.

Estate Tax Reporting and Potential Liability

In Illinois, estates that exceed certain value thresholds are subject to state and federal estate taxes. The real estate appraisal contributes to the estate's total value, which determines whether the estate meets tax-filing requirements. Executors are responsible for filing estate tax returns and should work with a tax advisor if the appraisal pushes the estate into taxable territory.

Asset Distribution Among Heirs

When multiple heirs are entitled to inherit the property or its value, the appraisal helps determine fair distribution. For example, if the estate includes both cash and real estate, some heirs may prefer to receive a cash equivalent rather than a property interest. The appraisal value provides a basis for calculating equitable shares and can help the executor avoid disputes among heirs.

Selling the Property in Probate

If the estate requires liquidation of assets to pay debts or distribute funds, the appraisal value serves as an objective starting point for listing the property. Executors working with a real estate agent can use the appraisal to establish an appropriate listing price, ensuring that the estate maximizes its return.

While probate properties are often sold "as-is," the appraised value can also help identify areas where minor improvements could increase the sale price without extensive investment.

Preparing for Potential Challenges or Disputes Over Value

In cases where beneficiaries disagree with the appraised value, or if they feel the property's worth affects their inheritance, the executor may face objections. Executors should be prepared to address these challenges calmly and objectively:

Communicating the Appraisal Process Clearly

Transparency is key to managing potential disputes. Executors should explain the appraisal process to beneficiaries and offer to share the report, helping them understand the methods used to determine value. Clear communication reassures heirs that the process is fair and unbiased.

Consulting with a Probate Attorney for Complex Situations

If there are strong objections to the appraisal or if the estate includes high-value or rare properties, consulting a probate attorney can be valuable. Attorneys can mediate discussions and help executors determine whether a second opinion is warranted. This approach prevents prolonged disputes and helps maintain trust among heirs.

Final Note: The Value of Professional Appraisal in Probate

Appraising real estate is an essential step in probate, impacting everything from tax filings to asset distribution. By selecting a qualified appraiser and approaching the process with transparency, executors fulfill their duty to provide an accurate, unbiased valuation. This appraisal not only satisfies Illinois probate requirements but also supports fair and equitable treatment of all beneficiaries. Executors who understand the role of appraisals can proceed with confidence, knowing that they have a reliable foundation for the real estate decisions that lie ahead in probate.

Market Analysis vs. Appraisal

In probate, understanding a property's value is crucial for informed decisions, whether the goal is selling, distributing to heirs, or retaining the property within the estate. While the formal appraisal discussed in Section 4.1 establishes the property's fair market value for legal and tax purposes, a **market analysis**—conducted by a real estate professional—offers additional insights specific to current market conditions and potential listing strategies.

This section will clarify the key differences between a market analysis and an appraisal, outline the unique advantages of each, and explain how these valuations serve different needs throughout probate. Executors can rely on both tools to balance court requirements with practical, market-driven strategies that maximize the estate's real estate value.

The Key Differences Between an Appraisal and a Market Analysis

Although appraisals and market analyses both assess a property's worth, their methods, purposes, and intended audiences differ significantly. Understanding these distinctions helps executors decide which tool is best suited for various probate tasks.

Purpose and Audience

- **Appraisal**: A formal appraisal is prepared by a licensed appraiser and establishes an unbiased, certified valuation of the property's fair market value. This value reflects what the property would reasonably sell for under normal market conditions and is typically used for official purposes, such as tax reporting, court documentation, and estate inventory. The primary audience for an appraisal includes the probate court, the IRS, and the estate's beneficiaries.

- **Market Analysis**: A market analysis, also called a **Comparative Market Analysis (CMA)**, is prepared by a licensed real estate agent and focuses on pricing the property to attract buyers. It compares the property to similar homes currently for sale or recently sold in the area, emphasizing real-time market trends, buyer interest, and strategic pricing. The main audience for a market analysis is the executor, beneficiaries, and potential buyers, as it provides actionable insights for listing the property effectively.

Methodology

- **Appraisal**: Appraisers rely on a standardized approach to valuation, analyzing the property's physical characteristics, its condition, and comparable sales. They provide detailed reports that document these factors and explain the methodology behind the valuation, ensuring that the final value is legally sound and defensible.

- **Market Analysis**: Real estate agents use local market knowledge and comparable property data to assess how the property aligns with buyer demand and neighborhood trends. Unlike appraisals, market analyses take into account buyer interest, current inventory, and seasonal factors that influence pricing, aiming to establish a competitive list price rather than an absolute market value.

When to Use an Appraisal vs. a Market Analysis in Probate

Each valuation serves a unique purpose in probate, and understanding when to use each tool can help executors meet both court and market needs effectively.

When an Appraisal is Required

Appraisals are generally required in probate for official purposes, particularly to:

- **Establish Tax Basis**: The appraisal sets the date-of-death value, which becomes the tax basis for the property. This value is essential for estate tax filings, inheritance tax assessments, and eventual capital gains calculations if the property is sold later.

- **Meet Court Requirements**: Illinois probate courts often require an appraisal to verify the property's fair market value, ensuring an accurate estate inventory.

- **Provide Transparency in Distribution**: When multiple heirs or beneficiaries are involved, an appraisal assures all parties that the property's value is determined objectively, preventing disputes over perceived undervaluation or favoritism.

For these reasons, an appraisal is best suited for establishing a legally recognized value that will be used for taxes, court filings, and impartial asset division among beneficiaries.

When a Market Analysis is Beneficial

While an appraisal establishes an official value, a market analysis is beneficial in probate when the estate plans to sell the property. A market analysis can help executors:

- **Set an Optimal Listing Price**: The real estate market fluctuates, and listing prices should reflect current demand, competitive listings, and the home's unique selling points. A market analysis provides the insights needed to price the property strategically for the current market.

- **Identify Property Enhancements**: Real estate agents conducting a market analysis can recommend minor updates or staging tactics that may increase appeal without significant investment. A CMA reveals what competing properties offer, guiding executors in making practical improvements.

- **Create an Effective Marketing Strategy**: Real estate agents use market analyses to develop listing strategies tailored to attract buyers in the property's price range, location, and condition. This proactive approach helps maximize the estate's return, often leading to faster sales and higher proceeds.

Executors should work with a probate-experienced real estate agent to benefit from an informed analysis of the current market, which can support effective listing decisions and ensure the estate gains the best possible financial outcome from the property sale.

How a Market Analysis Complements the Appraisal in Probate

In probate, both the appraisal and market analysis play important roles, and using them together provides a well-rounded perspective on the property's value.

Confirming Value and Market Feasibility

An appraisal provides the court and beneficiaries with a stable, court-approved value, while a market analysis offers flexibility based on present-day buyer trends. For example, if the appraisal indicates a higher value than the market analysis, executors may decide to price conservatively to ensure a timely sale, particularly if the estate must pay debts or distribute funds quickly.

Conversely, if the market analysis reveals a strong seller's market, the estate could list the property slightly above the appraisal value, potentially yielding higher proceeds for beneficiaries. Together, the two valuations give the executor a comprehensive picture that balances court compliance with market opportunity.

Informing Heirs and Preventing Disputes

Market analyses can also help executors manage expectations among beneficiaries. For heirs interested in selling the property quickly, a CMA provides evidence of the listing strategy's rationale, showing how the price aligns with market conditions. Sharing a market analysis alongside the appraisal helps prevent disagreements, as it clarifies why the executor is making specific pricing decisions and demonstrates a thorough approach to maximizing the property's potential.

Supporting Decisions on Property Improvements

A market analysis can guide cost-effective decisions on minor repairs or staging. If the appraisal confirms that the property holds substantial value, but the market analysis suggests that other homes in the area are more updated, the executor might invest in targeted improvements that yield a positive return on investment. Improvements guided by a CMA can help the property compete effectively with similar listings, often leading to quicker and more profitable sales.

Working with Professionals for Appraisals and Market Analyses

Choosing the right professionals for appraisals and market analyses can make a significant difference in probate outcomes. Executors should approach these services with care, as each requires specific expertise.

Licensed Appraisers for Court-Recognized Value

As discussed in Section 4.1, hiring a certified appraiser ensures that the valuation is credible, legally defensible, and acceptable to the probate court. Executors can rely on appraisers who specialize in probate properties, as they understand the legal context and can provide comprehensive reports that meet Illinois probate requirements.

Probate-Experienced Real Estate Agents for Market Analysis

A real estate agent with probate experience is invaluable when conducting a CMA, as they know how to approach probate properties and understand the importance of balancing financial goals with probate requirements. Experienced agents can also advise executors on practical listing strategies, taking into account probate timelines and any court approval processes necessary for the sale.

Collaborating with these professionals provides the executor with reliable data and insights tailored to the estate's needs, ensuring they make well-informed decisions that maximize the property's value for the estate.

Next Steps: Using Valuation Insights to Guide Estate Planning

Once both the appraisal and market analysis are complete, the executor has a solid foundation for moving forward. Here are a few actionable steps to consider:

Establish a Listing Strategy Aligned with Market Conditions

With a clear understanding of both the property's court-approved value and its market potential, the executor can develop a listing strategy. This might involve setting a competitive listing price, preparing the property for sale, or deciding whether to make minor improvements to increase buyer appeal.

Coordinate with Beneficiaries on Property Goals

The executor can share the results of the appraisal and market analysis with beneficiaries to set expectations and address any questions. When beneficiaries understand the basis for pricing and sale decisions, they are more likely to support the executor's approach, reducing the likelihood of disputes.

Finalize Tax and Court Documentation

With the appraisal value established, the executor can proceed with court documentation, tax filings, and inventory reporting, ensuring that all probate requirements are met. Having both valuations on hand makes it easier to complete these filings and address any questions from the probate court.

Final Note: Leveraging Both Tools for a Comprehensive Real Estate Strategy

In probate, a formal appraisal and a market analysis serve as complementary tools that help the executor navigate the complexities of real estate valuation and sale. While the appraisal fulfills the estate's legal requirements, a market analysis provides the flexibility to respond to current market conditions and attract the best possible offers. Executors who use both valuations are well-prepared to make informed, balanced decisions that uphold their fiduciary duty while maximizing the property's value for the benefit of the estate and its beneficiaries.

Understanding Illinois Inheritance and Estate Taxes

Inheriting property can create additional responsibilities beyond managing real estate. While the executor focuses on asset valuation and distribution, understanding the potential tax implications on the estate is essential for a complete and compliant probate process. Illinois has specific estate tax requirements that apply to estates above certain value thresholds, and while it does not impose an inheritance tax, federal estate taxes may apply to larger estates.

This section provides an overview of Illinois estate taxes, federal estate tax considerations, and how property appraisals impact these obligations. However, since tax matters can be complex and vary with each estate's unique circumstances, it's crucial to consult a qualified tax professional for advice. Following the "Who, not how" methodology, executors and beneficiaries are encouraged to work with tax experts to ensure proper filing and avoid unintended tax consequences.

Overview of Illinois Estate Tax

In Illinois, estates valued above a certain threshold may be subject to the state's estate tax, which is calculated separately from federal estate taxes. Executors should be aware of this threshold and understand how the total value of the estate, including real estate, affects tax responsibilities.

Illinois Estate Tax Threshold

At the time of publication, Illinois imposes estate tax on estates valued at $4 million or more, meaning that if the total estate value—including real estate, financial assets, and personal property—exceeds this amount, the estate may be subject to state taxes. Estates valued below $4 million are generally exempt from Illinois estate tax, but a complete valuation is still essential to determine whether the estate meets this threshold.

Illinois Estate Tax Rates

For estates exceeding $4 million, Illinois uses a progressive estate tax rate structure, with rates ranging from 0.8% to 16% of the estate's value over the threshold. The exact rate depends on the total value, so larger estates are taxed at higher rates. Executors can work with tax professionals to understand how these rates apply to the estate and calculate the estate's tax obligations accurately.

The Importance of Accurate Property Valuation

An accurate real estate appraisal, as discussed in Sections 4.1 and 4.2, is key to determining the estate's taxable value. Illinois estate tax is calculated based on the property's fair market value at the date of the decedent's passing, which the appraisal establishes. This appraisal forms the basis for tax calculations, inventory filings, and any capital gains considerations for heirs who inherit the property.

Federal Estate Tax Considerations

The federal estate tax operates separately from Illinois estate tax and has its own threshold and requirements. Executors should understand these distinctions, particularly if the estate's total value approaches or exceeds the federal estate tax exemption.

Federal Estate Tax Threshold

The federal estate tax exemption is currently much higher than Illinois's threshold, standing at $12.92 million In 2023 for individual estates. (This threshold is expected to decrease significantly in 2025, and changes frequently, so it is important to consult with a licensed tax professional for the most updated figures). Estates that exceed this amount may be subject to federal estate tax, which follows a progressive tax rate similar to Illinois but with a maximum rate of 40%.

Coordinating Federal and State Tax Filings

If the estate exceeds both Illinois and federal thresholds, the executor must coordinate state and federal tax filings. Each tax authority has its own deadlines, forms, and reporting requirements, and accurate filing is essential to avoid penalties or complications for beneficiaries. Due to the complexity of multi-level tax obligations, it's strongly recommended to consult a tax advisor who understands both Illinois and federal estate tax laws and can provide tailored advice.

Tax Implications for Heirs and Beneficiaries

Unlike estate taxes, which are paid by the estate itself, Illinois does not have an inheritance tax. However, inheriting property can have certain financial implications for beneficiaries, particularly related to future capital gains taxes.

Understanding the Step-Up in Basis

When heirs inherit real estate, they receive a "step-up" in basis, meaning the property's tax basis is adjusted to its fair market value at the date of the decedent's death. For example, if a home originally purchased for $100,000 is appraised at $300,000 at the time of inheritance, the heir's basis becomes $300,000. This adjustment minimizes potential capital gains taxes if the property is later sold, as only the difference between the sale price and the stepped-up basis is subject to capital gains.

Selling Inherited Property

If heirs decide to sell the inherited property, any appreciation beyond the stepped-up basis is subject to capital gains tax. For instance, if the property's basis is $300,000 and it later sells for $350,000, the taxable capital gain would be $50,000. Executors should inform beneficiaries about this potential tax impact and encourage them to seek advice from a tax professional to manage these implications effectively.

Preparing for Tax Filing and Payments

Proper tax planning is critical to meet all filing deadlines, avoid penalties, and ensure the estate remains compliant with Illinois and federal laws. Executors should take the following steps to facilitate an organized approach to tax matters:

Collecting Documentation for Accurate Reporting

Estate tax filings require comprehensive documentation, including the real estate appraisal, asset inventory, and any deductions or liabilities that impact the estate's taxable value. Executors can work with an accountant to ensure all required documentation is collected and organized, making it easier to complete filings accurately and on time.

Determining Filing Deadlines and Payment Schedules

Both Illinois and federal tax filings come with specific deadlines, typically nine months from the date of death for federal estate tax filings and within nine months for Illinois estate tax. If the executor anticipates delays, they may apply for extensions; however, any taxes owed are still due by the original deadlines. Collaborating with a tax professional helps ensure these timelines are met, preventing unnecessary penalties.

Funding Tax Payments Through Estate Assets

In cases where the estate owes substantial taxes, the executor may need to liquidate certain assets to cover these costs. Executors are empowered to use estate funds to pay taxes before distributions are made to beneficiaries, and in estates with high-value real estate, selling the property may be a practical solution. Executors should coordinate with financial advisors and real estate professionals to determine the best approach for managing tax payments.

Applying the "Who, Not How" Approach to Tax Matters

Navigating estate and inheritance tax requirements can be one of the most complex aspects of probate, especially when real estate is involved. Executors may feel pressured to find solutions on their own, but the "Who, not how" approach encourages relying on qualified professionals who can provide targeted expertise, rather than trying to master every aspect themselves. Consulting with a tax advisor, for instance, allows the executor to focus on administering the estate, while the tax advisor ensures compliance with all relevant tax obligations.

Engaging a Tax Professional for Compliance and Efficiency

Tax professionals with probate experience can advise on deductions, exemptions, and credits that may reduce the estate's tax burden, as well as clarify Illinois and federal requirements. Executors can rely on a tax expert to handle filings and payment scheduling, ensuring accuracy and minimizing the estate's liabilities.

Coordinating with a Probate Attorney

For executors facing substantial tax obligations or complex reporting requirements, probate attorneys can offer additional support by guiding the overall probate process, managing beneficiary communications, and ensuring tax filings align with Illinois probate court standards. This collaboration can ease the executor's burden, especially in estates with high-value assets or family members unfamiliar with probate's tax implications.

Final Note: The Importance of Professional Support in Tax Matters

Tax issues in probate require careful planning and attention to detail, particularly for Illinois estates that meet or exceed state and federal tax thresholds. Executors should approach these responsibilities with the understanding that while knowledge of tax basics is helpful, specific tax advice must come from qualified professionals. By following the "Who, not how" approach and seeking assistance from a tax advisor or probate attorney, executors can ensure the estate's tax obligations are met efficiently, ultimately protecting the estate's assets and fulfilling their fiduciary duty with confidence.

Summary

In Chapter 4, we explored the crucial steps involved in valuing real estate during probate, a process that impacts tax obligations, asset distribution, and potential property sales. Here are the key takeaways:

Appraisals Are Essential for Accurate Valuation: A formal appraisal establishes the fair market value of the property as of the decedent's passing, which is required for Illinois probate filings and estate tax purposes. An accurate appraisal provides an objective basis for inventory, helps calculate potential tax liabilities, and ensures fairness in distributions to heirs.

Market Analysis Complements the Appraisal: A Comparative Market Analysis (CMA) conducted by a real estate agent offers insights into current market conditions, guiding the executor on optimal listing strategies if the property will be sold. While the appraisal provides a legally recognized value, the market analysis helps set a realistic sale price based on buyer demand and competition in the local area.

Understanding Tax Implications is Crucial: Illinois estate tax may apply to estates exceeding $4 million, and federal estate tax could apply to larger estates above the federal threshold. Additionally, beneficiaries receive a "step-up" in tax basis on inherited property, which can reduce future capital gains taxes if they choose to sell. However, tax rules are complex, and executors should seek professional guidance to navigate these obligations effectively.

Overall, this chapter emphasizes the importance of accurate valuation and professional assistance. By understanding the distinct roles of appraisals and market analyses, as well as the tax considerations tied to real estate, executors can manage property effectively within probate and make decisions that best serve the estate and its beneficiaries.

Checklist: Key Steps for Preparing Real Estate for Sale in Probate

1. Making Decisions as a Family

☐ Open discussions with heirs and beneficiaries about the future of the property to reach a consensus on whether to sell, rent, or transfer ownership.

☐ Address any differing opinions, and consider holding a family meeting to discuss options, answer questions, and make decisions collectively.

☐ Consider consulting a probate attorney or mediator if family members have conflicting views that could delay or complicate the sale process.

☐ Document any agreed-upon decisions to ensure clarity and avoid misunderstandings later.

2. Assessing the Condition of the Property

☐ Conduct a thorough inspection of the property to evaluate its current condition and identify any issues that may need repair or maintenance.

☐ Decide if the property will be sold "as-is" or if certain repairs or upgrades will be made to increase market value.

☐ Get estimates for any recommended repairs or updates, such as fixing structural issues, updating outdated features, or addressing cosmetic improvements.

☐ Consider the cost-benefit of each repair to determine if the investment will lead to a higher sale price or faster sale.

3. Meeting Legal Obligations for Property Disclosure

☐ Review Illinois property disclosure requirements for probate sales to ensure full compliance.

☐ Prepare a disclosure statement that informs potential buyers of known issues, such as structural problems, environmental hazards, or other significant defects.

☐ If unsure about any disclosure requirements, consult with a probate attorney or real estate professional to confirm compliance with Illinois law.

☐ Be transparent about the property's condition to avoid potential disputes with buyers and ensure a smoother transaction.

4. Establishing Market Value with a Broker's Opinion

☐ Obtain a Comparative Market Analysis (CMA) from a probate-experienced real estate broker to determine a fair and competitive sale price for the property.

☐ Consider the broker's analysis of recent sales of comparable properties in the area, property condition, and current market trends.

☐ If necessary, arrange for a formal appraisal to validate the property's value, especially if required by the probate court or for estate accounting purposes.

☐ Work with the broker to establish an appropriate listing price that aligns with the estate's financial goals and market conditions.

Chapter 5

Preparing Real Estate For Sale

Deciding what to do with real estate in probate often involves important family discussions and practical considerations. This chapter focuses on preparing the property for sale, covering everything from family communication and assessing the property's condition to meeting legal disclosure obligations. In Illinois, selling real estate through probate requires an understanding of the property's market value and a thoughtful approach to deciding whether repairs or an "as-is" sale is best. By taking these steps, you can streamline the sale process and maximize the property's value, benefiting both the estate and its beneficiaries.

Making Decisions as a Family

One of the most challenging aspects of preparing probate real estate for sale is reaching a shared decision on the property's future among family members. When a loved one passes, family members may have differing emotional connections, expectations, and financial considerations tied to the property. Executors and family members must communicate openly about the next steps, whether that means preparing the property for sale, retaining it within the family, or considering alternatives. Clear and structured conversations can help prevent misunderstandings, foster consensus, and ensure that decisions align with the best interests of the estate.

In this section, we'll discuss strategies for effective family communication regarding probate property, along with tips for managing conflicts and reaching agreements that respect everyone's perspective.

Setting the Stage for Open Communication

The first step in making decisions as a family is establishing a respectful, open atmosphere where everyone feels comfortable expressing their thoughts. Emotions often run high following a loss, and family members may bring personal experiences and memories to these conversations, which can influence their perspectives. By approaching the discussion with empathy and understanding, executors and family members can create an environment conducive to honest dialogue.

Choosing the Right Time and Place

Setting aside a specific time and neutral location for these conversations helps avoid distractions and allows everyone to prepare. In-person meetings are ideal, but if family members live far apart, video calls can also provide a personal touch. Executors might also consider involving a neutral party, such as a Certified Real Estate Probate Specialist (C.P.R.S.) or a family mediator, if conversations become tense or difficult to manage.

Encouraging Transparency and Respect

Executors can help establish ground rules, such as letting each person speak without interruption and encouraging transparency about their feelings and concerns. Being open about the estate's needs, timelines, and legal requirements can help family members understand the responsibilities involved in preparing the property, ensuring everyone is aligned on the practicalities of the process.

Exploring Each Family Member's Perspective

Family members may have varied opinions on the property's future, from sentimental attachments to financial expectations. Understanding these perspectives can help identify common ground and clarify areas of disagreement, allowing the family to work toward a solution that honors the decedent's legacy.

Discussing Emotional and Financial Interests

For some family members, the property may hold significant sentimental value, especially if it was a family home or contained shared memories. Others may prioritize financial considerations, such as the proceeds from a sale, particularly if they have their own financial responsibilities. Executors should be prepared to listen to each viewpoint, recognizing that these perspectives are often deeply personal and valid.

Weighing All Options Together

Once everyone's thoughts have been shared, it can be helpful to list all potential options, including selling the property, keeping it within the family, or renting it out temporarily. Discussing these options in detail—including their financial, legal, and logistical implications—can bring clarity and guide the group toward a consensus.

Managing Conflicts and Resolving Disagreements

In probate situations, differing viewpoints can lead to tension or disagreements, especially if family members feel strongly about a particular outcome. Executors can play a key role in managing these conflicts by keeping conversations focused on the estate's goals and helping the family stay aligned with Illinois probate requirements.

Staying Neutral and Focusing on the Estate's Interests

Executors should aim to remain neutral, ensuring that decisions prioritize the estate's best interests. They can emphasize the fiduciary duty they hold to manage the estate objectively and follow Illinois probate law, which may help family members understand why certain decisions are necessary even if they aren't universally supported.

Involving a Third-Party Professional if Needed

If disagreements persist, family members may benefit from working with a probate mediator or a Certified Real Estate Probate Specialist (C.P.R.S.). These professionals can facilitate conversations and help the family find a balanced solution, providing an impartial perspective that respects everyone's interests while focusing on practical solutions.

Reaching a Consensus and Planning Next Steps

After discussing all viewpoints and exploring potential options, the family should aim to reach a consensus on the property's future. Once a decision has been made, clear next steps allow the executor to move forward confidently with preparing the property.

Confirming the Agreed-Upon Plan in Writing

Documenting the agreed-upon plan in writing helps prevent future misunderstandings and ensures that everyone is on the same page. A brief outline of the decision—whether to prepare the property for sale, retain it, or pursue an alternative—gives family members a clear record of what was discussed and agreed upon.

Establishing Roles and Responsibilities

If the family decides to sell or prepare the property, assigning specific roles can help streamline the process. For example, some family members may assist with decluttering and organizing the property, while others help coordinate repairs. Executors should communicate clearly about the tasks required and keep everyone informed of progress, timelines, and any changes to the plan.

Final Thoughts: The Value of Professional Guidance in Family Decisions

Making decisions about a probate property can be an emotionally charged process, but clear communication and a structured approach can help family members find a path forward that respects everyone's interests. By fostering open dialogue, exploring each person's perspective, and involving professional guidance when needed, executors can navigate these conversations with confidence. Working with a Certified Real Estate Probate Specialist (C.P.R.S.) ensures that family decisions align with Illinois probate requirements and allows the family to prepare the property effectively, setting the stage for a smooth and successful sale or transfer.

Evaluating the Condition of the Property

Once a consensus is reached on selling the property, the next step in preparing real estate for sale in probate is to evaluate its condition. Many probate properties may have been lived in for years with minimal updates or upkeep, and determining the property's current state is crucial to deciding whether to sell it "as-is" or make cost-effective improvements. A thorough assessment of the property allows the executor to weigh the benefits and costs of repairs and updates, all while considering the best interests of the estate.

In this section, we'll look at the process of evaluating the property's condition, including professional inspections, prioritizing necessary repairs, and deciding on updates that may improve buyer appeal without overextending the estate's funds.

Conducting a Thorough Property Assessment

To establish a realistic view of the property's current state, executors should begin with a thorough assessment of its interior and exterior. Probate properties often require additional attention due to deferred maintenance, and understanding any underlying issues early on can prevent surprises during the sale process.

Using a Professional Home Inspection

A professional home inspection can reveal the true condition of the property, from structural elements like the roof and foundation to essential systems such as plumbing, electrical, and HVAC. This inspection provides the executor with a detailed report, highlighting issues that might deter buyers or result in costly negotiations. Identifying these factors upfront enables executors to decide if any repairs are needed to preserve the estate's value.

Documenting the Property's Condition

Keeping a record of the property's current state is important for transparency in probate. This documentation, which may include inspection reports, photos, and notes on visible issues, helps the executor demonstrate due diligence in managing the property. In Illinois, accurate records can support disclosure requirements and provide evidence of any actions taken to address maintenance or repair issues.

Weighing the Pros and Cons of Selling "As-Is"

Selling a property "as-is" means listing it in its current condition without making repairs or upgrades. For many probate properties, this approach can simplify the process, especially if the estate's funds or timeline do not allow for extensive improvements. However, an "as-is" sale also has its drawbacks, including potential price reductions to compensate for the property's condition.

Benefits of an "As-Is" Sale

Selling a probate property "as-is" can be an efficient choice, particularly if the property requires significant repairs or if the estate's financial resources are limited. With an "as-is" sale, buyers understand that they are purchasing the property in its current condition, and the executor avoids upfront repair costs, labor, and time delays.

Potential Drawbacks of an "As-Is" Sale

While an "as-is" sale simplifies the preparation process, it may attract fewer buyers or result in lower offers, as buyers may anticipate additional expenses for repairs. Some prospective buyers may expect a discount that reflects the cost of addressing deferred maintenance or updating the property to meet current market standards. Executors should consider these factors carefully when deciding whether to pursue an "as-is" sale or make minor improvements.

Identifying and Prioritizing Essential Repairs

If the executor decides to make some improvements, the focus should be on essential repairs that address health, safety, or structural issues. These repairs can increase buyer confidence and potentially attract higher offers, even if the property is otherwise being sold "as-is."

Focusing on Health and Safety Repairs

Repairs related to health and safety—such as fixing electrical hazards, repairing water leaks, and addressing mold or pest issues—are often necessary to make the property habitable and appealing to buyers. These improvements protect the property's value and make it more marketable by removing potential red flags that may discourage prospective buyers.

Managing Minor Cosmetic Repairs

While cosmetic updates are generally optional, some minor repairs, such as fixing broken fixtures, patching walls, or replacing worn carpet, can improve the property's presentation without substantial expense. These small fixes can make the home feel more inviting and well-maintained, helping it stand out to buyers without a major investment.

Budgeting for Repairs

Executors should carefully evaluate the costs of any repairs to avoid overextending the estate's funds. Consulting a real estate agent or Certified Real Estate Probate Specialist (C.P.R.S.) can provide insight into which repairs are likely to yield a positive return, ensuring that the estate's resources are used efficiently.

Determining Value-Enhancing Updates

While probate properties don't usually require extensive remodeling, some targeted updates can enhance buyer appeal and marketability. Executors should consider these updates only if they align with the estate's financial interests and if they are likely to yield a positive return in the sale.

Enhancing Curb Appeal

A property's exterior creates the first impression, and small improvements to curb appeal can attract more buyers. Basic landscaping, such as mowing the lawn, trimming hedges, and adding fresh mulch, can make a significant difference. Executors may also consider minor exterior updates, such as repainting the front door or replacing outdated fixtures, to improve the property's appearance without major expense.

Low-Cost Interior Updates

Inside the property, small upgrades like painting walls in neutral colors, replacing old light fixtures, or installing new hardware can modernize the space and make it more appealing. These low-cost updates create a clean, move-in-ready impression, allowing potential buyers to envision themselves in the home.

Weighing the Benefits of Updates with Market Insights

Executors should carefully weigh the cost of any updates against their potential return, considering local market conditions and buyer expectations. Consulting with a real estate professional or C.P.R.S. can help the executor determine which updates are worthwhile and avoid improvements that may not substantially increase the property's value.

Preparing for Disclosure Requirements

Illinois law requires full disclosure of the property's known condition, especially when selling probate properties. Executors should be aware of these requirements and prepared to share information on any known issues, as well as any repairs made. Transparent disclosure helps protect the executor from potential liabilities and ensures that buyers have a clear understanding of the property's condition.

Documenting All Repairs and Updates

Executors should keep detailed records of any repairs or updates made, including receipts, contractor invoices, and inspection reports. This documentation is helpful for disclosure requirements and provides transparency for both the probate court and potential buyers.

Preparing for Buyer Inquiries

Buyers may have questions about the property's history, condition, and any work completed. Executors who are prepared to answer these questions transparently can facilitate a smoother sale process and build buyer confidence. Open communication about the property's condition reassures buyers and reduces the likelihood of unexpected issues arising after the sale.

Final Thoughts: Balancing Condition with Market Goals

Evaluating the condition of a probate property is an essential step in preparing it for sale. By carefully assessing the property's current state, considering the pros and cons of an "as-is" sale, and prioritizing cost-effective repairs, executors can make decisions that serve the estate's best interests. Working with a Certified Real Estate Probate Specialist (C.P.R.S.) provides valuable insights into which updates will enhance the property's appeal and help executors navigate the balance between market expectations and probate requirements. A well-prepared property not only attracts more buyers but also supports a smooth, successful sale that honors the decedent's legacy and benefits all heirs and beneficiaries.

Legal Obligations for Disclosure

In Illinois, sellers—including executors of probate estates—are legally required to disclose certain details about a property's condition to prospective buyers. These disclosures protect buyers by providing transparency about known issues with the property, allowing them to make informed decisions. For executors, understanding these disclosure obligations is essential for ensuring compliance with Illinois real estate laws and reducing the risk of potential liabilities after the sale. In probate cases, where the executor may have limited firsthand knowledge of the property, fulfilling disclosure requirements can be challenging, but taking the proper steps helps protect both the estate and prospective buyers.

This section outlines the key disclosure obligations in Illinois probate real estate sales, including the legal requirements, the process of completing disclosure forms, and best practices for transparency with buyers.

Understanding Illinois Real Estate Disclosure Requirements

Illinois law requires sellers to disclose any known material defects or issues with the property that could affect its value or safety. These requirements apply to all residential property sales, including those in probate. Executors should be aware that even though they may not have lived in or have detailed knowledge of the property, they are still obligated to disclose any known issues based on the information available.

Completing the Residential Real Property Disclosure Report

The Illinois Residential Real Property Disclosure Act requires sellers to complete a disclosure report that lists various aspects of the property, such as structural integrity, plumbing, electrical systems, and environmental hazards. Executors must fill out this report to the best of their knowledge, noting any known defects or repairs, even if they personally have not used or occupied the property.

Relying on Inspection and Documentation

Because executors often lack firsthand experience with the property, they may rely on recent inspection reports, appraisals, or records from the decedent to identify known issues. While executors are not expected to uncover hidden problems, they must disclose all known information about the property's condition. Professional inspections, as discussed in previous sections, can be invaluable for revealing issues that should be included in the disclosure report.

Common Disclosure Items for Probate Properties

Probate properties often have specific issues due to their age, deferred maintenance, or extended vacancy. Executors should be prepared to disclose any of the following common issues if they are known to affect the property's condition.

Structural and Foundation Issues

Structural integrity is one of the key elements in the disclosure report. Executors should note any known issues with the foundation, walls, or roof. For example, cracks in the foundation, leaks, or signs of shifting can impact the property's stability and may be required to be disclosed if known.

Plumbing, Electrical, and HVAC Systems

The condition of essential systems like plumbing, electrical wiring, and HVAC should be disclosed if known, as these can be costly repairs for buyers. Executors who have obtained an inspection report will have detailed information on these systems, allowing them to accurately oomploto this part of the disclosure

Environmental Hazards and Safety Concerns

Illinois disclosure laws require sellers to inform buyers of any known environmental hazards, such as mold, asbestos, lead-based paint, or radon, as these can impact both health and property value. Executors should pay particular attention to any hazards identified in inspection reports and include these in the disclosure.

Pest or Infestation Issues

Properties that have been vacant for extended periods are more susceptible to pest issues, such as termites, rodents, or other infestations. Executors should disclose any known pest problems, as well as any treatments or extermination efforts taken to address these issues.

Best Practices for Transparency and Buyer Confidence

Disclosures are an essential tool for building buyer trust and ensuring a smooth sale. By being transparent, executors help prospective buyers make informed decisions, reducing the likelihood of disputes or legal complications after the sale. Here are some best practices for ensuring full transparency:

Being Forthcoming About the Property's History

If the property has a history of repairs or updates, executors should include this information in the disclosure. Providing accurate records and documents, such as past repair receipts, inspection reports, and warranty information, helps buyers understand the property's maintenance history.

Consulting a Probate Attorney for Compliance

Given the legal responsibilities of disclosure, consulting with a probate attorney can be beneficial. An attorney can help review the disclosure report for accuracy and compliance with Illinois law, ensuring that all necessary information is provided and reducing the risk of potential liabilities for the executor.

Disclosing Known Limitations of Knowledge

Executors may not have complete knowledge of the property's condition, and it's acceptable to indicate this on the disclosure form when appropriate. If certain areas of the property's history or condition are unknown, executors can note these limitations transparently, which is better than leaving details incomplete or guessing.

Documenting Disclosures and Repairs for Court Records

Keeping a record of all disclosures, inspection reports, and repair documents is essential for probate court compliance. Detailed documentation protects the executor and the estate from future claims, showing that the sale was handled with transparency and due diligence.

Maintaining a Disclosure Record

Executors should keep a copy of the completed disclosure report, along with any inspection findings, receipts for repairs, and other relevant documents. This record provides a clear trail of actions taken and can be referenced if questions arise during probate court proceedings or by beneficiaries.

Including Disclosure Documentation in Final Estate Records

Including all disclosure-related documentation in the estate's final records demonstrates that the executor has fulfilled their fiduciary duty, helping reassure the probate court and beneficiaries that the property was sold ethically and transparently. This thorough approach can help prevent challenges or objections from heirs who may be unfamiliar with the property's true condition.

Final Thoughts: Ensuring Full Compliance with Illinois Disclosure Laws

For executors, fulfilling disclosure obligations is a crucial part of preparing probate real estate for sale. While they may not have lived in the property, executors are still responsible for disclosing all known information about the property's condition to comply with Illinois law and protect the estate from future liabilities. By taking the time to complete disclosures accurately, consulting a probate attorney as needed, and being transparent with buyers, executors can facilitate a smoother sale process. Ensuring that the property's known condition is clearly communicated to potential buyers builds trust, safeguards the estate, and upholds the executor's fiduciary responsibilities.

Establishing Market Value
with a Broker's Opinion

Once the property is prepared and disclosure requirements are met, the next step in selling real estate through probate is establishing an accurate listing price. This is where a broker's opinion, typically delivered as a **Comparative Market Analysis (CMA)**, becomes invaluable. A CMA provides a detailed overview of how the probate property compares to other properties in the area, helping executors set a realistic and competitive price based on current market conditions. Given the distinct nature of probate sales, relying on a CMA conducted by a probate-experienced real estate agent helps executors ensure the property is priced to attract interested buyers while safeguarding the estate's financial interests.

In this section, we'll cover how a CMA is conducted, the factors it considers, and the benefits it provides to executors managing a probate sale in Illinois.

Understanding the Role of a Comparative Market Analysis (CMA)

A Comparative Market Analysis is a report prepared by a licensed real estate broker or agent that estimates a property's fair market value by comparing it to recently sold and active listings of similar properties. For probate properties, where pricing may be influenced by unique circumstances, a CMA offers an objective, data-driven foundation for establishing an appropriate listing price.

Comparing Similar Properties in the Area

A CMA focuses on "comparables," or similar properties in the area that have recently sold or are currently listed. The analysis typically considers factors like the property's location, square footage, age, and condition. For a probate property, the agent may select comparables with similar age or condition, particularly if the property is being sold "as-is."

Evaluating Local Market Trends

The CMA also provides insight into broader market trends, such as whether it's a buyer's or seller's market, how long similar properties stay on the market, and current pricing strategies. This context helps executors gauge how competitively their property can be positioned and gives realistic expectations for the time it may take to sell.

Factors a Broker Considers in a CMA

A CMA goes beyond listing comparable properties; it assesses various property characteristics and market dynamics to arrive at a suggested listing range. Probate properties often require specific considerations, especially if they differ from typical market-ready homes. Here are the primary factors a broker evaluates in a CMA for probate real estate:

Property Condition and Necessary Adjustments

A property's condition significantly influences its market value. If the probate property requires repairs or has been listed "as-is," the CMA will take this into account by comparing it to similar homes in comparable conditions. The broker may make adjustments to reflect any essential repairs or deferred maintenance, balancing these factors against properties with updated or well-maintained features.

Location and Neighborhood Characteristics

Location is a core factor in determining property value, including the neighborhood's desirability, proximity to schools, amenities, and market demand in the area. Properties in high-demand neighborhoods tend to fetch higher prices, while those in less competitive areas may require price adjustments to attract buyer interest. The broker's local expertise helps executors understand how location impacts the estate's market value.

Market Dynamics and Seasonal Trends

Real estate markets fluctuate seasonally and can be influenced by broader economic conditions. A broker conducting a CMA will consider recent shifts in buyer demand, average time on market, and any seasonal trends that could affect pricing. For instance, probate properties may sell more quickly in a competitive spring or summer market but require price adjustments during slower seasons.

The Benefits of a CMA in Probate Sales

For executors, a CMA provides clarity and confidence in setting a price that aligns with market expectations and the estate's goals. Here's how a CMA helps manage the probate sale effectively:

Establishing a Competitive and Realistic Price

One of the CMA's main advantages is setting a listing price that reflects true market conditions. Overpricing can result in a property sitting on the market for extended periods, which could lead to price reductions and reduced buyer interest. A CMA ensures the property is competitively priced from the start, increasing the likelihood of a timely sale that benefits the estate and its beneficiaries.

Supporting Executor Decisions and Court Requirements

An accurate CMA provides executors with a data-backed basis for their pricing decision, which can be valuable if the price needs to be justified to beneficiaries or the probate court. Executors who document their reliance on a CMA demonstrate that they've acted with due diligence, supporting their fiduciary duty to make financially sound decisions on behalf of the estate.

Reducing the Risk of Over- or Underpricing

A CMA also protects against the risks of overpricing or underpricing. For probate properties, which may have unique challenges compared to traditional listings, a well-researched CMA reflects the property's true market value. This approach prevents the estate from losing potential

133

profits through underpricing or from losing buyer interest through overpricing.

Working with a Probate-Experienced Real Estate Agent

A CMA is most effective when prepared by a real estate agent who understands the probate process and market conditions specific to probate properties. Working with a probate-experienced agent ensures the CMA is tailored to the property's unique features and the estate's goals.

Leveraging Probate-Specific Market Knowledge

A probate-experienced agent is familiar with the challenges that probate properties often face, such as deferred maintenance, limited disclosures, or as-is conditions. This knowledge allows the agent to select appropriate comparables and recommend a price that accurately reflects the property's condition and market appeal.

Gaining Local Insight for a Smooth Sale

Local expertise is essential in real estate, particularly for probate properties where minor pricing adjustments can make a big difference in attracting buyers. A probate-experienced agent provides insights into how local buyer preferences and recent sales trends can influence pricing, helping executors set a price that aligns with current demand.

Reviewing and Adjusting the Price as Needed

Real estate markets are dynamic, and it's not uncommon for listing prices to require adjustment based on buyer feedback or changes in market conditions. Executors should be prepared to review and adjust the price if necessary, especially if the property does not attract buyer interest within the expected timeframe.

Monitoring Buyer Interest and Market Feedback

During the listing period, the executor and agent can track buyer inquiries, showing activity, and feedback to gauge the property's reception in the market. If buyer interest is lower than anticipated, a price adjustment might be warranted to attract more prospective buyers.

Reevaluating Price Based on Market Conditions

External factors, such as economic shifts or seasonal slowdowns, may impact the property's saleability. Executors should stay flexible and consider adjusting the price based on current conditions, with the guidance of their agent, to increase the chances of a timely sale.

Final Thoughts: Setting the Stage for a Successful Sale with a CMA

For probate properties, establishing the right listing price is key to balancing market appeal with the estate's financial goals. A Comparative Market Analysis (CMA) prepared by a probate-experienced agent provides an objective, market-driven foundation for setting a realistic price. By using a CMA to inform their pricing strategy, executors can move forward confidently, knowing they've fulfilled their duty to manage the estate's assets responsibly. A well-priced probate property is more likely to attract serious buyers, paving the way for a smoother, successful sale that meets the needs of both the estate and its beneficiaries.

Summary

In Chapter 5, we covered the essential steps for preparing probate real estate for sale, from making initial family decisions to establishing a competitive market value. Here are the main points covered in this chapter:

1. **Making Decisions as a Family**: Open communication among family members is crucial when deciding the future of probate property. By discussing everyone's perspectives and reaching consensus, families can move forward with a plan that respects the decedent's legacy and addresses each member's expectations.

2. **Evaluating the Condition of the Property**: Assessing the property's current condition helps executors decide whether to sell "as-is" or make select repairs. Executors are encouraged to prioritize necessary health and safety repairs, balance the cost of minor improvements, and document the property's state to ensure transparency with potential buyers.

3. **Legal Obligations for Disclosure**: Illinois law requires executors to disclose known issues about the property's condition. Executors are responsible for completing a disclosure report based on available information, ensuring buyers have a clear understanding of the property and reducing the risk of post-sale disputes.

4. **Establishing Market Value with a Broker's Opinion**: A Comparative Market Analysis (CMA) conducted by a probate-experienced real estate agent provides an objective basis for setting a competitive listing price. The CMA considers comparable properties, local market trends, and the probate property's specific features, helping executors attract buyers and achieve a sale that serves the estate's interests.

Together, these steps equip executors to prepare probate real estate thoughtfully and effectively, ensuring compliance with Illinois probate law, protecting the estate's value, and creating a smoother path to a successful sale.

Checklist: Key Steps for Preparing Real Estate for Sale in Probate

1. Making Decisions as a Family

- ☐ Hold discussions with heirs and beneficiaries to reach a consensus on the future of the property (sell, rent, or retain within the family).
- ☐ Address any differing opinions among family members and consider consulting a mediator or probate attorney if there are conflicts that could delay or complicate the process.
- ☐ Document the agreed-upon decision to provide clarity and prevent misunderstandings as you move forward with the sale.
- ☐ Assign roles and responsibilities if family members will be involved in tasks like repairs, cleaning, or property management.

2. Assessing the Condition of the Property

- ☐ Conduct a thorough inspection of the property, noting any repairs or maintenance needs that might affect marketability or buyer interest.
- ☐ Decide whether to sell the property "as-is" or invest in specific repairs or updates that could improve its value or appeal.
- ☐ Obtain estimates for necessary repairs or updates, such as fixing structural issues, addressing safety hazards, or making minor cosmetic improvements.
- ☐ Evaluate the cost-benefit of each repair, considering how it could impact the sale price and the speed of the sale.

3. Meeting Legal Obligations for Property Disclosure

- ☐ Review Illinois property disclosure requirements, as probate properties must still meet all state regulations for disclosure.
- ☐ Prepare a disclosure statement to inform potential buyers of known issues with the property, such as structural defects, environmental hazards, or past water damage.
- ☐ If there is any uncertainty about disclosure requirements, consult a probate attorney or real estate professional familiar with Illinois law to ensure full compliance.
- ☐ Ensure transparency in the property's condition to avoid potential disputes and legal issues with buyers.

4. Establishing Market Value with a Broker's Opinion

☐ Contact a probate-experienced real estate broker to conduct a Comparative Market Analysis (CMA) to determine a competitive listing price for the property.

☐ Review the broker's analysis, which should consider recent comparable sales, the current market, and the condition of the property.

☐ If required by the probate court or if an accurate valuation is critical, arrange for a formal appraisal to validate the property's value.

☐ Work with the broker to set a listing price that aligns with the estate's financial goals and the needs of the beneficiaries, considering both market conditions and the property's appeal.

Chapter 6

The Probate Sales Process

Selling real estate in probate involves several unique steps and requirements, including listing the property, working with a probate-experienced agent, and seeking court approval for offers. In Illinois, the probate sale process is designed to ensure fairness and transparency for all involved parties. This chapter provides a step-by-step guide to listing the property, accepting offers, negotiating terms, and gaining court confirmation, helping you manage the sale with confidence and compliance. By understanding this process, you'll be well-prepared to handle the sale effectively and maximize the estate's returns.

Listing the Property

Once the property has been prepared, evaluated, and priced, the next step in the probate sale process is listing it on the market. For executors, listing a probate property involves additional considerations beyond a standard sale, from fulfilling legal requirements to managing the expectations of beneficiaries and potential buyers. A well-executed listing not only attracts buyers but also ensures that the probate process remains transparent and compliant with Illinois probate laws. Understanding the steps involved in listing helps executors set the stage for a smooth and successful sale.

This section outlines how to prepare a probate property for listing, what executors can expect once it's on the market, and the importance of staying organized and communicative throughout this critical stage.

Final Preparations for Listing

Before the property goes live on the market, executors should confirm that all necessary preparations have been completed. This includes ensuring the property's condition meets market expectations (based on any prior repairs or upgrades), reviewing and finalizing disclosure documents, and gathering all relevant paperwork related to the property.

Verifying Disclosure Documents and Records

As discussed in previous sections, Illinois law requires executors to disclose known material defects or conditions affecting the property. Executors should review these documents with their real estate agent to confirm accuracy, ensuring the disclosures are complete and ready for prospective buyers. Keeping these records organized will streamline communication with interested parties and demonstrate the executor's due diligence to both the court and beneficiaries.

Staging and Presenting the Property

While probate properties don't always need extensive staging, presenting a clean, well-maintained space can enhance buyer interest. Minor touches like deep cleaning, decluttering, and adding a few simple staging elements can make the property feel more inviting. Executors should work with their agent to identify cost-effective ways to highlight the home's best features while keeping the process efficient.

Setting Up the Listing with the Probate-Experienced Agent

Listing a probate property on the market requires specific expertise, as these sales often have unique considerations that differ from typical real estate transactions. A probate-experienced agent understands these differences and can help navigate the listing process effectively.

Crafting a Transparent and Compliant Listing Description

Probate properties are often listed with additional transparency to manage buyer expectations, especially if the property is being sold "as-is" or if certain disclosures are required. The agent can help craft a listing description that accurately reflects the property's condition, any recent updates, and details that might appeal to the buyer demographic most likely interested in probate properties. The listing description should be factual and compliant with all Illinois real estate advertising standards.

Deciding on Listing Channels and Marketing Strategy

A probate-experienced agent will determine the best channels to list the property and tailor a marketing strategy to attract the right buyers. Probate properties can be marketed to appeal to investors, first-time buyers, or buyers looking for unique homes, depending on the property's characteristics. A targeted marketing approach increases visibility and attracts serious buyers, ultimately benefiting the estate.

Managing Buyer Interest and Communication

Once the property is listed, executors should be prepared to manage inquiries from potential buyers. Probate listings may receive varying levels of interest depending on the property's price, condition, and market conditions, and staying organized is key.

Preparing for Buyer Questions and Showing Requests

Because probate properties can involve unique conditions or disclosures, buyers may have additional questions. Executors should work closely with their agent to ensure they're prepared to respond to questions about the probate process, the property's condition, and any specific requirements for the sale. For buyers interested in touring the property, organizing a showing schedule that accommodates beneficiaries' and family members' needs can help streamline the process and avoid conflicts.

Keeping Beneficiaries Informed

Executors have a fiduciary duty to keep beneficiaries informed of major developments in the sale. Regular updates about the listing status, offers received, and potential buyer feedback help maintain transparency and reduce misunderstandings. Beneficiaries who are informed of the progress are more likely to support the executor's decisions, especially if they understand the challenges or delays that may arise in a probate sale.

Handling Offers and Preparing for Court Involvement

When offers begin to come in, it's important for executors to understand that probate sales in Illinois may require court approval before an offer can be finalized. While the next section will go into greater detail on accepting offers and court confirmation, it's useful to be aware of this aspect of probate sales from the outset.

Reviewing Offers with the Agent's Guidance

A probate-experienced agent can assist executors in reviewing offers and determining which offer best aligns with the estate's needs. The agent can provide advice on evaluating offer terms, buyer qualifications, and any contingencies that may complicate the sale. Executors should be prepared for the possibility of accepting an offer conditionally, pending court approval.

Preparing for Court Confirmation

In Illinois, probate courts may need to confirm or approve the sale before it can close. Executors should familiarize themselves with the court's requirements, including necessary documentation and timelines. Working closely with the agent and a probate attorney ensures that all steps are completed promptly, paving the way for a smoother court confirmation process.

Final Thoughts: The Importance of Organization and Clear Communication in Listing

Listing a probate property is a multi-step process that requires careful coordination, transparency, and compliance with Illinois probate laws. By working with a probate-experienced agent, executors can ensure the property is presented effectively to the market and that disclosures, pricing, and showing arrangements meet legal and market standards. Staying organized, communicating with beneficiaries, and anticipating court involvement all contribute to a more efficient and successful listing phase, setting the estate up for a well-managed sale.

Working with a Qualified Real Estate Professional

Successfully selling real estate in probate requires more than basic real estate knowledge; it demands expertise in both the probate process and the unique challenges that probate properties often present. A Certified Real Estate Probate Specialist (C.P.R.S.) provides this specialized knowledge, guiding executors through each stage of the sale with probate-specific skills and strategies. A C.P.R.S. is not only well-versed in Illinois probate laws and court requirements but is also trained to manage the often-sensitive nature of probate sales, from communicating with beneficiaries to addressing unique property conditions. This certification ensures that the agent has the experience and training necessary to navigate the complexities of probate real estate and meet the expectations of both the court and potential buyers.

This section outlines the advantages of working with a C.P.R.S., detailing how they support executors through listing, marketing, and negotiating the sale in compliance with Illinois probate requirements.

Specialized Knowledge of Probate Requirements

A Certified Real Estate Probate Specialist understands the specific legal and procedural requirements that govern probate property sales. This specialized training prepares them to handle tasks unique to probate, such as court-required disclosures, court confirmations, and fiduciary responsibilities to the estate and beneficiaries.

Ensuring Compliance with Illinois Probate Law

One of the greatest advantages of working with a C.P.R.S. is their understanding of Illinois probate law. They are familiar with the documentation and disclosures needed to comply with the Illinois Probate Act and can help executors manage these requirements smoothly. A C.P.R.S. ensures that all necessary steps are followed, reducing the likelihood of legal complications that could delay the sale or create liability for the executor.

Managing Court Approval Requirements

In Illinois, probate property sales may require court confirmation, especially when multiple beneficiaries or high-value assets are involved. A C.P.R.S. is familiar with these court requirements and can guide the executor through the confirmation process, preparing the necessary documentation and ensuring deadlines are met. This expertise streamlines the sale process and provides peace of mind that all procedural requirements are being addressed properly.

Expertise in Marketing Probate Properties

Selling a probate property requires a tailored marketing approach to attract the right buyers. Unlike traditional listings, probate properties may appeal to a specific demographic, such as investors or buyers seeking properties with unique histories or characteristics. A C.P.R.S. uses probate-specific marketing strategies to reach these buyers while setting realistic expectations about the sale's parameters.

Creating a Transparent and Accurate Listing

A C.P.R.S. knows how to position the property with a listing description that balances transparency with buyer appeal. This includes providing clear, factual information about the property's condition, noting any "as-is" requirements, and including disclosures that comply with Illinois law. A well-crafted listing helps manage buyer expectations, reducing the risk of deal complications later in the process.

Utilizing Targeted Marketing Channels

A C.P.R.S. understands which marketing channels are most effective for probate properties and can design a strategy that appeals to likely buyers, such as real estate investors or first-time buyers looking for unique opportunities. By targeting marketing efforts, a C.P.R.S. maximizes exposure and attracts serious, qualified buyers who are ready to navigate the probate sale process.

Setting an Informed and Competitive Price

A C.P.R.S. is trained in evaluating the market value of probate properties, taking into account their specific challenges and unique features. This expertise is critical for setting a realistic price that aligns with the estate's financial goals and court requirements while appealing to buyers.

Providing a Data-Driven Comparative Market Analysis (CMA)

A C.P.R.S. can prepare a Comparative Market Analysis (CMA) that reflects current market trends and the property's characteristics, including its condition and the probate sale context. By using probate-relevant comparables and market data, a C.P.R.S. helps the executor establish a fair listing price that attracts buyers without compromising the estate's value.

Avoiding Overpricing and Underpricing Risks

For probate properties, pricing correctly is essential to prevent the property from sitting on the market too long or, conversely, selling below its true value. A C.P.R.S. uses their expertise to set a price that balances market demands with the estate's interests, reducing the risk of costly pricing errors and ensuring the estate is managed responsibly.

Managing Communication with Beneficiaries and Buyers

Probate sales often involve multiple parties with vested interests, including heirs, beneficiaries, and potential buyers. A C.P.R.S. understands the sensitivity required in probate transactions and can facilitate communication in a way that supports transparency and builds trust.

Keeping Beneficiaries Informed

One of the C.P.R.S.'s roles is to keep beneficiaries updated on the sale's progress. By providing regular updates and explaining how each step serves the estate's interests, a C.P.R.S. helps maintain harmony and alignment among family members, minimizing potential disputes over the sale.

Addressing Buyer Questions and Concerns

Probate sales often generate specific questions from buyers, who may be unfamiliar with the probate process or concerned about the property's condition. A C.P.R.S. is prepared to answer buyer inquiries about disclosures, sale conditions, and court approval timelines, facilitating a smoother transaction and addressing buyer concerns upfront.

Guiding Executors Through the Offer and Negotiation Process

Once offers start coming in, a C.P.R.S. helps the executor evaluate each offer carefully. They bring negotiation skills and probate-specific knowledge to the table, ensuring that offers are considered in light of both the estate's goals and the legal requirements governing probate sales.

Evaluating Offers Based on Estate Objectives

A C.P.R.S. assists executors in reviewing offers not just for price, but also for buyer qualifications, contingencies, and terms that could impact the sale timeline. This guidance ensures that the executor considers offers holistically, balancing the estate's financial goals with court compliance needs.

Negotiating for Fair Terms in a Probate Sale

Negotiating a probate sale can be complex, as it may involve multiple stakeholders and legal considerations. A C.P.R.S. knows how to negotiate effectively within this context, securing fair terms while remaining sensitive to the needs of both the estate and beneficiaries.

Final Thoughts: The Value of a Certified Real Estate Probate Specialist

Working with a Certified Real Estate Probate Specialist (C.P.R.S.) provides executors with the specialized support and guidance needed to manage the probate sale process effectively. From ensuring compliance with Illinois probate requirements to creating a targeted marketing strategy and managing communication, a C.P.R.S. brings invaluable expertise to each stage of the sale. For executors, partnering with a C.P.R.S. not only simplifies the probate process but also ensures that the property's sale is handled professionally, ethically, and in the best interests of the estate and its beneficiaries.

Accepting Offers and Court Confirmation

Once the probate property is listed and starts receiving interest, the next phase involves reviewing offers and, in most cases, securing court approval before the sale can be finalized. In Illinois, probate property sales often require court confirmation, especially when multiple beneficiaries are involved or when the property represents a significant portion of the estate's value. For executors, understanding this two-part process—accepting an offer and obtaining court approval—is essential for moving forward confidently and ensuring the sale aligns with Illinois probate requirements.

In this section, we'll cover what executors need to know about evaluating offers, accepting the best offer for the estate, and navigating the court confirmation process.

Reviewing and Accepting Offers

The first step in moving toward a sale is reviewing all offers received and determining which one best serves the estate's goals. Since probate properties often attract a range of buyers, including investors, first-time homebuyers, and those seeking "as-is" opportunities, it's important to evaluate each offer carefully. Executors should look beyond just the offer price, considering other terms and contingencies that may impact the sale's outcome.

Evaluating Offers with Professional Guidance

With the help of a Certified Real Estate Probate Specialist (C.P.R.S.), executors can evaluate offers based on price, buyer qualifications, contingencies, and any specific conditions that could complicate the transaction. For example, a cash offer from a well-qualified buyer may be preferable to a higher offer with extensive contingencies. By weighing all aspects of each offer, the executor can make an informed decision that maximizes the estate's financial outcome and minimizes risks.

Choosing the Offer That Best Serves the Estate

When selecting an offer, it's essential to choose one that aligns with the estate's needs, the beneficiaries' expectations, and the court's requirements. A strong offer will balance fair market value with terms that support a smooth, timely sale. Executors should also ensure that the selected offer has the flexibility to move through the probate process without creating delays or complications.

Preparing to Accept the Offer

Once an offer is chosen, the executor, in consultation with the C.P.R.S., will proceed with the formal steps of accepting it. This typically involves notifying all parties, finalizing the sale contract, and preparing documentation for court review if necessary. This stage is key for transitioning into the court confirmation phase.

Understanding the Court Confirmation Process

In Illinois, probate courts play an essential role in overseeing the sale of estate property, ensuring that all transactions are fair and in the estate's best interest. Court confirmation is a way of safeguarding the estate and providing a layer of oversight to protect beneficiaries and creditors. Executors should be prepared to navigate this process with the support of their C.P.R.S. and, if necessary, a probate attorney.

Submitting the Accepted Offer for Court Approval

To obtain court confirmation, the executor must submit the accepted offer, along with the necessary supporting documentation, to the probate court. This documentation typically includes a summary of the offer's terms, details about the marketing process, and an explanation of why the selected offer is beneficial for the estate. The court will review this information to ensure the sale aligns with the estate's fiduciary obligations and meets any applicable legal standards.

Attending the Court Confirmation Hearing

In most cases, the court will schedule a confirmation hearing where the executor, beneficiaries, and sometimes even potential buyers can attend. During this hearing, the court will review the offer and determine if it meets the requirements to proceed. If there are no objections from beneficiaries or other interested parties, the court will likely approve the sale. However, in cases where multiple beneficiaries or creditors are involved, the court may hear concerns or review additional evidence before making a final decision.

Addressing Potential Objections

Sometimes, beneficiaries or other interested parties may object to the sale or the selected offer. In these instances, the executor, with guidance from the C.P.R.S. and possibly a probate attorney, should be prepared to present the reasoning behind the offer's selection. Transparent documentation of the listing process, marketing efforts, and evaluation criteria can be instrumental in demonstrating that the chosen offer was in the estate's best interest and that the executor acted in good faith.

Finalizing the Sale After Court Approval

Once the court confirms the sale, the executor can proceed with the closing process. This final stage requires coordination with the buyer, the C.P.R.S., and potentially a probate attorney to ensure all conditions are met and the sale concludes smoothly.

Completing the Closing Process

The closing process for probate property is similar to that of a standard real estate transaction but with additional steps to meet probate compliance. The executor, with the C.P.R.S.'s support, will oversee the closing, ensuring all documents are signed, funds are distributed according to the court's directives, and the transfer of ownership is legally finalized. At this stage, the estate receives the sale proceeds, which will then be used to satisfy any remaining debts before distribution to beneficiaries.

Distributing Sale Proceeds to the Estate

After the sale is completed, the proceeds are returned to the estate and are used to settle any outstanding debts, taxes, or probate expenses. The remaining funds are then prepared for distribution according to the decedent's will or Illinois intestacy laws if no will exists. Executors should keep clear records of these transactions, as they may be required to submit final accounting documentation to the court and beneficiaries.

Communicating with Beneficiaries Throughout the Process

Clear communication with beneficiaries is essential at every stage of accepting offers and obtaining court confirmation. Executors should keep beneficiaries informed of the offer status, upcoming court hearings, and any potential challenges in the confirmation process. Transparent communication helps maintain trust among family members and ensures they understand the executor's commitment to acting in the estate's best interest.

Providing Updates on Key Milestones

Regular updates, particularly when the offer is accepted and when the court confirmation is scheduled, help beneficiaries stay engaged and informed. Sharing milestones and explaining any delays or additional requirements keeps expectations realistic and prevents misunderstandings.

Addressing Concerns and Managing Expectations

If beneficiaries have concerns about the offer, pricing, or court confirmation, the executor, with the C.P.R.S.'s support, should be prepared to address these questions openly. This can help manage expectations and reassure beneficiaries that every effort is being made to maximize the estate's value and honor the decedent's intentions.

Final Thoughts: Navigating Offers and Court Confirmation with Care

Accepting an offer and obtaining court confirmation are two pivotal steps in the probate sale process. With guidance from a Certified Real Estate Probate Specialist (C.P.R.S.), executors can evaluate offers strategically, ensuring that the best terms are selected for the estate. The court confirmation process, while sometimes complex, provides essential oversight to protect the estate's interests and give beneficiaries peace of mind. By approaching these stages carefully, executors can move toward a successful sale that honors the estate's goals, complies with Illinois probate requirements, and benefits all parties involved.

Negotiating in Probate Sales

Negotiating the sale of a probate property has unique challenges that require balancing the estate's financial goals with the specific limitations and conditions common in probate. Unlike typical real estate transactions, probate sales often involve stricter disclosure requirements, "as-is" conditions, and potential court oversight, which can all impact negotiation strategies. Executors must carefully navigate these factors to ensure that the final sale terms align with the estate's objectives and comply with Illinois probate requirements.

With the assistance of a Certified Real Estate Probate Specialist (C.P.R.S.) to guide the process, executors can approach negotiations with strategies tailored to the probate context, creating a smoother path to closing.

Setting Expectations with "As-Is" Conditions

Many probate properties are sold "as-is," meaning the estate does not intend to make repairs or improvements before selling. This approach can attract certain buyers, such as investors, but it also requires clear communication from the outset to prevent misunderstandings during negotiation.

Reinforcing the "As-Is" Condition

To avoid potential conflicts, executors should ensure that the "as-is" condition is clearly stated in the listing and confirmed during negotiations. Buyers who understand this up front are less likely to request extensive repairs, and setting these expectations early helps streamline the process. If a buyer requests concessions for specific repairs, the executor can consider price adjustments rather than actual repairs, which keeps the estate's out-of-pocket expenses to a minimum.

Considering Price Adjustments or Credits

In some cases, providing a modest price reduction or repair credit can be more beneficial than outright rejecting requests. A small adjustment

153

might preserve buyer interest and support a faster closing, especially if the property has been on the market for some time. Executors should consider these requests strategically, weighing the benefit of a quicker sale against the estate's overall financial goals.

Navigating Common Buyer Contingencies

Buyer contingencies—such as inspection, financing, and appraisal conditions—are common in any real estate transaction, but they can pose unique challenges in probate sales. Executors should understand the potential impact of these contingencies and work to negotiate terms that maintain a balance between buyer needs and estate objectives.

Handling Inspection Contingencies

If a buyer's offer includes an inspection contingency, the executor may need to negotiate on any issues the inspection reveals. For probate properties sold "as-is," executors can approach these contingencies by offering credits or minor price adjustments rather than agreeing to repairs. This approach respects the "as-is" condition while still keeping the sale moving forward.

Evaluating Financing Contingencies

Financing contingencies are another common factor, particularly if the buyer is securing a mortgage. Since probate properties sometimes appeal to cash buyers, executors may prioritize offers without financing contingencies, as cash sales often reduce the time and complexity of closing. However, if a financing-contingent offer is the best available option, the executor should confirm that the buyer is pre-approved and capable of completing the sale within a reasonable timeframe.

Preparing for Appraisal Requirements

When financing is involved, the property may need to meet the lender's appraisal requirements. If the appraisal comes in below the agreed-upon sale price, the executor may need to negotiate with the buyer to bridge the gap. Executors can consider a slight price reduction if this aligns with the estate's objectives, but they should also assess if waiting for another buyer might yield a higher net outcome for the estate.

Responding to Buyer Offers Strategically

When negotiating a probate sale, it's essential to evaluate each offer based on both the price and terms, as different offers may carry varying levels of risk and benefit for the estate. Executors should weigh the strengths of each offer beyond just the dollar amount to ensure a smooth and compliant transaction.

Choosing Offers with Stronger Terms

In probate, offers that include fewer contingencies, stronger buyer qualifications, or shorter closing timelines are often more attractive than those that offer a higher price but come with potential delays. Executors should consider the net benefits of each offer, particularly if a lower offer could result in a faster, more efficient sale that meets the estate's objectives.

Remaining Flexible and Open to Counteroffers

Probate sales can involve additional steps that delay closing, and buyers may seek certain accommodations in response. Executors who remain open to reasonable counteroffers or minor concessions—such as adjusting the closing date or providing limited credits—can often move negotiations forward while still meeting the estate's financial goals.

Managing Communication and Transparency with Beneficiaries

Throughout the negotiation process, executors must also keep beneficiaries informed of any significant developments, particularly if adjustments to the sale price or terms are being considered. Clear communication not only maintains trust but also provides transparency regarding the executor's actions and rationale.

Providing Regular Updates

Executors should update beneficiaries on the negotiation progress, especially if terms are being modified. This can include explaining why certain concessions were made or detailing any adjustments in the expected sale timeline. Keeping beneficiaries informed reassures them that the sale is being handled responsibly and in their best interest.

Addressing Beneficiary Concerns

Beneficiaries may have questions or concerns about the negotiation strategy, especially if offers vary significantly in terms. Executors should be prepared to answer questions about why certain decisions were made and how the chosen negotiation strategy aligns with the estate's objectives. Open communication fosters understanding and reduces the potential for disputes after the sale.

Final Thoughts: Negotiating Probate Sales with Care and Strategy

Negotiating a probate sale requires a thoughtful approach, balancing the unique requirements of probate with the estate's financial goals. By maintaining clear communication, carefully managing buyer contingencies, and staying flexible in response to offers, executors can navigate this complex phase with confidence. Working alongside a Certified Real Estate Probate Specialist (C.P.R.S.), executors are better equipped to handle the nuances of probate negotiation, ensuring a sale that benefits the estate and satisfies all parties involved.

Summary

In Chapter 6, we outlined the essential steps of navigating a probate property sale, from listing the property to finalizing offers and managing negotiations. Here are the key takeaways:

1. **Listing the Property**: Executors began by listing the probate property, ensuring it was accurately presented with clear disclosures. This included preparing for buyer inquiries and setting realistic expectations about the "as-is" condition or any known issues. A well-organized listing phase helps set the property up for a smoother sale process.

2. **Working with a Certified Real Estate Probate Specialist (C.P.R.S.)**: Partnering with a C.P.R.S. provided specialized expertise, ensuring that the probate sale complied with Illinois probate requirements and attracted the right buyers. A C.P.R.S. guided executors through each stage, from marketing to evaluating offers, making the process more efficient and informed.

3. **Accepting Offers and Court Confirmation**: Executors learned the importance of carefully reviewing offers, considering terms and contingencies beyond just the sale price. Once an offer was selected, the next step often involved obtaining court confirmation. This legal oversight ensured that the sale was in the best interest of the estate and protected all beneficiaries.

4. **Negotiating in Probate Sales**: Negotiating a probate sale requires a tailored approach, as probate properties may involve unique conditions, such as "as-is" sales and specific buyer contingencies. Executors, supported by their C.P.R.S., balanced these considerations with the estate's goals, addressing buyer requests strategically and remaining transparent with beneficiaries throughout the process.

In summary, Chapter 6 highlighted the importance of careful planning, communication, and probate-specific expertise. By following these steps, executors are equipped to manage the probate sale process effectively, resulting in a fair, compliant sale that maximizes value for the estate and meets the needs of all parties involved.

Checklist: Key Steps for the Probate Sale Process

1. Listing the Property for Sale

☐ Prepare the property for listing by completing any necessary repairs, cleaning, and staging to enhance its appeal.

☐ Gather required documents for listing, including the property's title, any appraisal or market analysis, and disclosure forms.

☐ Choose a real estate broker with probate experience to guide the listing process, ensuring familiarity with Illinois probate requirements.

☐ Confirm the listing price with the broker, taking into account the property's market value, condition, and comparable sales in the area.

2. Working with a Probate-Experienced Agent

☐ Verify that the agent has experience handling probate sales and understands Illinois probate rules and procedures.

☐ Discuss the agent's marketing strategy for probate properties, including how they plan to attract buyers and handle any probate-specific questions.

☐ Ensure the agent is comfortable with court requirements, deadlines, and documentation needed for probate real estate transactions.

☐ Establish clear communication channels with the agent to stay updated on showings, offers, and feedback from potential buyers.

3. Accepting Offers and Court Confirmation

☐ Review any offers with the agent, taking into account price, contingencies, and buyer qualifications.

☐ Understand that in Illinois probate sales, court confirmation may be required before a sale can be finalized, especially if beneficiaries or heirs are involved.

☐ Work with the agent to select the best offer and prepare for the court approval process.

☐ Notify all interested parties and beneficiaries of the accepted offer and upcoming court confirmation, as required by Illinois probate law.

4. Negotiating in Probate Sales

☐ Recognize that negotiations in probate sales may involve additional steps, as buyers may be less familiar with the probate process.

☐ Be prepared to negotiate contingencies, repairs, or other terms to meet both buyer and court expectations.

☐ Ensure that any changes or negotiated terms are documented thoroughly and submitted to the court, if required, to maintain transparency.

☐ Confirm that all parties understand the unique aspects of the probate sale, including timelines, conditions, and court requirements, to prevent misunderstandings or delays.

Chapter 7

Handling Special Situations in Probate Real Estate

Every probate case is unique, and certain situations require additional care and expertise. In this chapter, we'll address special circumstances that can arise in probate real estate, such as disputes among heirs, properties with outstanding mortgages, and handling distressed or vacant properties. These situations can add complexity and may impact the probate timeline, but with the right knowledge and approach, executors can manage them effectively. This chapter offers guidance on navigating these challenges while protecting the estate's value and ensuring a fair process for all beneficiaries.

Managing Heir Disputes and Conflicts

Disputes among heirs are unfortunately common in probate, particularly when it comes to decisions about real estate. For many families, a loved one's home is not only a financial asset but also an emotional one, often carrying sentimental value or representing a significant portion of the estate. These factors can lead to conflicting opinions on whether to keep, sell, or divide the property, and disagreements can complicate the probate process if not managed carefully. Executors play a crucial role in resolving these disputes fairly and transparently, as they are legally responsible for ensuring that the estate is handled in the best interest of all beneficiaries.

This section provides guidance for executors on managing heir conflicts, including strategies for remaining neutral, facilitating open communication, and bringing in third-party support when necessary. By approaching these situations thoughtfully, executors can help prevent disputes from derailing the probate process and ensure that all heirs feel their perspectives have been heard.

The Executor's Role in Managing Heir Disputes

As the appointed representative of the estate, the executor has a fiduciary duty to manage estate assets impartially, in compliance with Illinois probate law. This means making decisions that reflect the best interests of the estate and all beneficiaries. In cases of heir disputes, an executor's role is to remain neutral, gather and share relevant information, and ensure that all decisions are guided by the decedent's will or Illinois intestacy laws, if no will exists.

Remaining Impartial

To maintain credibility and trust, the executor should approach every decision from a place of neutrality. This can be particularly challenging if the executor is also a family member, as they may have their own emotional ties to the property or opinions on what should happen. Staying focused on fulfilling the decedent's wishes, as outlined in the will, or abiding by Illinois probate law helps the executor avoid appearing biased, which can reduce the likelihood of conflict.

Focusing on Fulfilling the Decedent's Wishes

If a valid will exists, the executor's primary responsibility is to execute the decedent's instructions regarding the property. In cases where the will explicitly states what should be done with the real estate, this can simplify the process by providing a clear directive. However, even when the will's instructions are clear, heirs may have emotional reactions or differing interpretations, making it important for the executor to keep communication open and encourage all parties to focus on honoring the decedent's wishes.

Facilitating Open Communication Among Heirs

Clear, consistent communication is key to managing heir disputes and preventing misunderstandings. Executors can play an active role in keeping heirs informed of the probate process, property status, and any updates or decisions being made. By creating an open channel for dialogue, executors can help prevent small misunderstandings from escalating into larger conflicts.

Scheduling Family Meetings or Updates

Holding family meetings, either in person or virtually, allows heirs to discuss their perspectives, ask questions, and receive updates directly from the executor. This forum encourages transparency and gives each heir an opportunity to voice concerns or ideas. If emotions run high, it may be helpful to set ground rules for respectful communication and designate time for each person to share their views.

Keeping Records of All Communications

Documenting discussions and key decisions made in meetings or through written updates helps ensure that there is a record of the executor's efforts to remain transparent. Providing written summaries of these meetings and distributing them to heirs offers a reference for later, reducing the potential for claims of miscommunication or favoritism.

Encouraging Compromise and Flexibility

In cases where heirs disagree on major decisions—such as whether to keep or sell the property—the executor can encourage heirs to consider various options or compromises. For example, some heirs may be willing to buy out others, or the property might be sold with proceeds divided among beneficiaries. Executors should make it clear that any agreement must serve the estate's best interest and meet probate requirements.

Bringing in Professional Mediation or Legal Support

When heir disputes cannot be resolved through open communication, bringing in third-party professionals may be necessary to facilitate resolution. Professional mediators and probate attorneys can offer impartial perspectives and help family members reach agreements that honor the estate's goals without further straining family relationships.

Engaging a Probate Mediator

Probate mediators specialize in resolving family conflicts in estate matters. They are trained to guide discussions, manage emotions, and facilitate constructive conversations. Executors can suggest mediation when disputes seem too entrenched for family-led discussions, as a mediator's neutral position can help all parties feel heard and respected.

Consulting with a Probate Attorney

If disagreements continue to impact the probate process, a probate attorney can provide legal guidance on how to proceed in compliance with Illinois law. Attorneys can advise on the executor's obligations, help clarify beneficiaries' rights, and, if necessary, represent the estate in court. This legal expertise is invaluable in situations where heir disputes could delay or jeopardize the probate timeline.

Knowing When to Seek Court Intervention

In extreme cases, the probate court may need to intervene to resolve disputes. While court involvement can be time-consuming and potentially divisive, it ensures that decisions are made impartially and according to Illinois probate law. Executors should consider this as a last resort, as court intervention can be costly and may further strain family relationships. However, it may be the most appropriate course if all other efforts to reach a resolution have failed.

Communicating the Executor's Fiduciary Responsibility

Executors may encounter situations where heirs pressure them to make decisions that would not align with the estate's best interest or legal obligations. It's essential for executors to remind heirs that their primary duty is to the estate, not to any one individual's preferences.

Emphasizing the Executor's Legal Duty

Executors should remind heirs that they are legally bound to act in a way that benefits the estate as a whole. Communicating this responsibility can help set expectations and clarify why certain decisions are made, even if they may not align with one heir's wishes. Executors can explain that their actions are guided by the will, Illinois probate law, and their fiduciary duty to all beneficiaries equally.

Providing Transparency on Financial Decisions

To maintain trust, executors should be transparent about how financial decisions are made, including any repairs, taxes, or costs associated with preparing the property for sale. Detailed financial records and regular updates demonstrate that decisions are made objectively and in the estate's best interest, reducing the potential for conflict.

Final Thoughts: Navigating Heir Disputes with Care and Professional Support

Managing heir disputes in probate can be challenging, but with clear communication, impartiality, and a focus on fulfilling the decedent's wishes, executors can help prevent conflicts from derailing the probate process. By facilitating open dialogue, encouraging compromise, and seeking third-party support when needed, executors create a more collaborative environment for resolving disagreements. Working with a Certified Real Estate Probate Specialist (C.P.R.S.) and consulting legal professionals can further support executors in handling these sensitive situations responsibly and fairly, ensuring that the estate's goals are met and that the probate process moves forward smoothly.

Properties with Outstanding Mortgages

In probate, it's common for executors to encounter properties with existing mortgages. When a decedent's property has an outstanding mortgage, the executor must decide how to handle this debt while managing the probate process. Unlike other estate assets, real estate often comes with financial obligations that must be addressed to prevent foreclosure or other legal complications. Executors have a fiduciary responsibility to protect the property's value and ensure the mortgage is managed effectively, whether through continued payments, refinancing, or selling the property.

This section provides guidance on handling a probate property with an outstanding mortgage, exploring the options available to executors to fulfill this responsibility while keeping the estate's best interest at the forefront.

Understanding the Executor's Responsibility for the Mortgage

When the decedent's property has an outstanding mortgage, the executor is responsible for ensuring that mortgage payments are made throughout the probate process. This prevents the property from going into default or foreclosure, which could jeopardize its value and complicate the estate's distribution. Executors should assess the property's mortgage terms and explore all options available to meet the estate's obligations.

Continuing Monthly Mortgage Payments

If the estate has sufficient liquid assets, the executor may choose to continue making monthly mortgage payments until the property is sold or otherwise distributed. Regular mortgage payments help maintain the property's standing with the lender and prevent late fees or penalties. However, if the estate lacks liquidity, alternative options may need to be considered.

Communicating with the Lender

Executors should contact the mortgage lender as soon as possible to inform them of the decedent's passing and confirm the mortgage's current status. Some lenders may offer temporary forbearance options, allowing payments to be postponed until the property is sold. Communicating openly with the lender ensures the executor understands the lender's requirements and any available options for managing the mortgage during probate.

Exploring Options for Paying Off the Mortgage

If the estate has sufficient funds or other assets, paying off the mortgage in full may be a viable option. Doing so eliminates monthly obligations and can simplify the process of selling or distributing the property. Executors should consider the estate's financial situation and discuss options for paying off the mortgage with a probate attorney or financial advisor if necessary.

Using Estate Assets to Satisfy the Mortgage

Executors may use estate funds or other liquid assets to pay off the mortgage balance, provided this approach aligns with the decedent's wishes and the estate's financial goals. Paying off the mortgage can be beneficial if it simplifies the distribution process, reduces interest expenses, or allows the property to be sold more easily. However, it's important for executors to balance this decision with the need to cover other estate obligations.

Refinancing the Mortgage in the Heir's Name

In some cases, an heir may wish to keep the property and assume responsibility for the mortgage. If the lender allows, refinancing the mortgage in the heir's name may be an option, enabling the property to transfer ownership without requiring the estate to cover the full mortgage balance. Executors should consult with both the heir and the lender to understand any requirements or eligibility criteria for refinancing under this arrangement.

Selling the Property to Satisfy the Mortgage

Selling a probate property with an outstanding mortgage is often the most practical solution, especially if the estate lacks the funds to cover ongoing payments or the heirs do not wish to assume the mortgage. In this scenario, the sale proceeds can be used to pay off the mortgage balance, with any remaining funds distributed according to the will or Illinois intestacy laws.

Determining the Property's Market Value and Mortgage Balance

Before proceeding with a sale, executors should determine both the property's current market value and the outstanding mortgage balance. This information will help assess whether the sale will generate enough funds to satisfy the mortgage and cover other estate expenses. If the property's value exceeds the mortgage balance, the estate can benefit from the remaining proceeds after the debt is settled.

Navigating a Short Sale if the Property is Underwater

In some cases, the property's market value may be less than the outstanding mortgage balance, a situation known as being "underwater." If this occurs, the executor may need to negotiate a short sale with the lender, in which the lender agrees to accept less than the full balance to avoid foreclosure. Short sales require the lender's approval and can be a complex process, but they allow the estate to avoid foreclosure and move forward with closing the property.

Communicating with Heirs and Beneficiaries

Handling a property with an outstanding mortgage often requires difficult decisions, especially if it means selling the property or using estate funds to cover the debt. Executors should keep heirs and beneficiaries informed of the mortgage status, options considered, and the reasoning behind each decision to maintain transparency.

Setting Realistic Expectations

Executors should communicate openly with heirs about the implications of the mortgage on the estate's overall finances. If a sale is necessary to pay off the mortgage, discussing this in advance can help manage expectations and avoid misunderstandings. Executors can explain that the decision to sell is based on protecting the estate's value and fulfilling their fiduciary duty.

Offering Options to Interested Heirs

If an heir expresses a desire to keep the property, executors should discuss the potential of refinancing the mortgage in the heir's name or arranging a buyout. While these options depend on the heir's financial standing and the lender's policies, exploring alternatives can provide a sense of empowerment and cooperation among beneficiaries.

Preparing for the Court's Oversight

In Illinois, probate courts may require documentation of the mortgage status and any decisions made regarding the property. Executors should be prepared to provide clear records to the court, particularly if they choose to use estate assets to pay off the mortgage or pursue a sale.

Keeping Detailed Financial Records

Executors should maintain thorough records of all mortgage payments, communications with the lender, and any financial decisions related to the mortgage. These records will be necessary if the court requests an accounting of how estate funds were used, especially if the mortgage is paid off using other assets within the estate.

Documenting the Sale Process

If the property is sold to satisfy the mortgage, executors should document each step of the sale, including the listing, negotiation, and closing stages. This documentation demonstrates that the sale was handled transparently and in the estate's best interest, helping executors fulfill their legal responsibilities.

Final Thoughts: Managing Outstanding Mortgages in Probate

Dealing with a property that has an outstanding mortgage requires careful consideration of the estate's resources and the decedent's wishes. Executors have several options, from continuing monthly payments to selling the property, each with its own implications for the estate's finances. By staying in communication with the lender, exploring solutions with beneficiaries, and documenting each decision, executors can manage the mortgage responsibly while protecting the estate's value. A Certified Real Estate Probate Specialist (C.P.R.S.) or probate attorney can further support executors in navigating these options, ensuring the property is handled effectively and in compliance with Illinois probate law.

Dealing with Liens and Judgments

When a probate property has outstanding liens or judgments, these encumbrances must be addressed before the property can be sold or transferred to heirs. Liens and judgments can arise from unpaid debts, taxes, or court orders, and they create a legal claim on the property. Executors are responsible for identifying any liens or judgments on the estate's real estate assets and working to resolve them in compliance with Illinois probate law. Clearing these encumbrances is essential to protect the estate's value and ensure a successful sale or transfer to beneficiaries.

This section provides guidance on handling liens and judgments, including how to identify these issues, the steps to clear them, and strategies for managing complex cases.

Identifying Liens and Judgments on the Property

The first step in handling liens or judgments on a probate property is to identify any existing encumbrances. Executors should conduct a thorough title search to ensure that all liens, judgments, and other claims on the property are accounted for.

Conducting a Title Search

A title search provides a detailed history of the property's ownership and financial encumbrances, such as liens, judgments, or unpaid property taxes. Executors can work with a title company or attorney to perform a title search and obtain a title report. This report reveals any claims on the property that must be resolved before a transfer or sale, giving the executor a full picture of the property's legal status.

Reviewing Types of Liens and Judgments

Different types of liens and judgments can affect a property, each with its own requirements for resolution. Common types include property tax liens, mechanic's liens for unpaid contractor work, and judgment liens from court orders. Executors should understand the nature of each lien, as this affects the steps required to clear it. For instance, tax liens generally need to be paid in full, while other liens may have negotiation options.

Prioritizing Liens and Resolving Outstanding Debts

Once liens and judgments are identified, the executor must prioritize them according to Illinois law. Certain liens, such as property tax liens, often take priority and must be cleared before others. Understanding this hierarchy helps the executor manage debts effectively and avoid complications that could delay the probate process.

Addressing Property Tax Liens

Property tax liens are a top priority, as they represent the government's legal claim to unpaid taxes. These liens can lead to a tax sale if left unresolved. Executors should contact the county tax assessor's office to determine the amount owed and arrange for payment from estate funds. Clearing property tax liens ensures that the estate avoids legal penalties and protects the property's ownership status.

Resolving Mechanic's and Contractor Liens

Mechanic's liens are filed by contractors or suppliers for unpaid labor or materials used on the property. These liens can often be negotiated if the parties involved agree to a reduced payment. Executors should reach out to contractors or lien holders directly or work with an attorney to negotiate terms. Settling these liens promptly can help prevent disputes and facilitate the sale process.

Paying Off Judgment Liens

Judgment liens arise from court-ordered debts or damages and can be attached to a property to secure payment. These liens typically require payment in full, though some creditors may agree to a settlement. Executors can work with a probate attorney to assess the best course of action for clearing judgment liens, especially if the creditor is open to negotiation.

Exploring Payment Options for Clearing Liens

Clearing liens and judgments can be financially challenging, particularly if the estate has limited liquid assets. Executors have several options for resolving these debts, including using estate funds, negotiating settlements, or using proceeds from a property sale.

Using Estate Funds to Clear Liens

If the estate has sufficient liquid assets, executors may choose to pay off liens and judgments directly. This option simplifies the sale process by removing encumbrances upfront, making the property more attractive to buyers. Executors should document all payments and ensure that these funds are allocated according to the estate's priorities.

Negotiating Settlements

In some cases, creditors may be willing to accept a reduced amount to clear a lien or judgment, especially if a quick resolution is beneficial to both parties. Executors can negotiate directly with lienholders or seek assistance from a probate attorney to discuss possible settlements. Negotiating a lower payment can preserve more estate funds for other expenses or distributions to heirs.

Clearing Liens Through Sale Proceeds

If estate funds are insufficient to cover the liens and judgments, executors may need to sell the property and use the proceeds to satisfy these debts. In such cases, the liens are typically paid off directly from the sale proceeds at closing. Executors should work with a title company to ensure that all encumbrances are addressed in the closing process, allowing for a clear transfer of title to the buyer.

Preparing for Court Approval and Documentation

In Illinois, probate courts may require executors to provide documentation of how liens and judgments were handled as part of the final estate accounting. Executors should keep detailed records of all payments, negotiations, and communication with lienholders, as this documentation is essential for court review and for maintaining transparency with beneficiaries.

Documenting All Payments and Negotiations

Executors should retain records of all lien payments, settlement agreements, and correspondence with creditors. This includes receipts, payment confirmations, and any written agreements for reduced payments. Comprehensive documentation demonstrates that the executor fulfilled their duty to manage the estate's debts responsibly and protects the executor from potential disputes.

Reporting to the Court and Beneficiaries

As part of the probate process, executors may need to submit an accounting to the court detailing how estate funds were used to clear liens and judgments. Providing this report to both the court and beneficiaries ensures transparency and helps prevent misunderstandings. Executors should work closely with a probate attorney if they need assistance preparing these reports to comply with Illinois probate requirements.

Final Thoughts: Clearing Liens and Judgments in Probate Real Estate

Managing liens and judgments on a probate property requires careful organization, prioritization, and negotiation. By conducting a thorough title search, understanding each lien's requirements, and exploring payment options, executors can address these encumbrances efficiently and protect the property's value. Keeping clear documentation and maintaining transparency with the court and beneficiaries are essential steps to ensure the probate process proceeds smoothly. Executors can seek guidance from a Certified Real Estate Probate Specialist (C.P.R.S.) or probate attorney to handle complex cases, ensuring that all liens and judgments are managed responsibly and in accordance with Illinois law.

Vacant or Distressed Properties

In probate, it's common for properties to be vacant for extended periods or to show signs of neglect and disrepair. Vacant or distressed properties present unique challenges, from security risks and maintenance concerns to reduced market appeal. Executors are responsible for managing these challenges to protect the property's value and to prepare it for eventual sale or distribution. Properly securing, assessing, and deciding on the best course of action for vacant or distressed properties helps prevent legal liabilities and maximize the estate's assets.

This section covers key considerations for executors handling vacant or distressed properties, including securing the property, evaluating repair needs, deciding whether to sell "as-is," and managing any additional expenses that may arise.

Securing and Protecting a Vacant Property

Vacant properties can be vulnerable to vandalism, theft, weather damage, and general deterioration. Executors should prioritize securing the property to protect it from these risks, as damages or liabilities arising from an unsecured property can impact the estate's overall value and delay the probate process.

Changing Locks and Securing Entry Points

One of the first steps is to change the locks and ensure all windows, doors, and other entry points are secured. By doing so, the executor can control access to the property and reduce the risk of unauthorized entry. If family members or heirs need access, the executor can create a controlled process for entry to minimize potential security issues.

Installing Security Measures

If the property will be vacant for an extended period, additional security measures may be beneficial. Executors might consider installing a security system, cameras, or even temporary alarms to deter vandalism or theft. In some cases, a simple monitoring service can provide peace of mind by regularly checking on the property's condition.

Informing Local Authorities

For added security, executors can notify local law enforcement or neighbors of the property's vacant status, which encourages extra vigilance. Police departments in some areas may perform periodic checks on vacant properties, helping prevent vandalism or break-ins.

Maintaining the Property's Condition

A vacant property requires ongoing maintenance to prevent deterioration and maintain curb appeal. By managing basic upkeep, executors can help retain the property's value and make it more appealing to potential buyers if it's listed for sale.

Regular Landscaping and Exterior Care

Simple exterior maintenance, such as mowing the lawn, trimming overgrown vegetation, and clearing debris, helps the property avoid an abandoned look, which can attract vandalism and reduce its curb appeal. Executors can arrange for landscaping services to maintain the property's exterior, making it look well-kept and more inviting to buyers.

Addressing Weather-Related Risks

Vacant properties are especially vulnerable to weather damage, particularly in Illinois, where seasonal changes can bring severe conditions. Executors should ensure that the property's HVAC system is appropriately adjusted, pipes are insulated to prevent freezing, and gutters are cleared to prevent water damage. These basic precautions help prevent costly repairs that could affect the estate's value.

Conducting Periodic Inspections

Scheduling regular inspections allows the executor to monitor the property's condition, identify any issues, and address them before they worsen. These inspections can reveal minor repairs that may prevent larger problems down the line, such as leaks, pest infestations, or structural concerns.

Deciding Whether to Sell "As-Is" or Make Repairs

When preparing a vacant or distressed property for sale, executors must weigh the costs and benefits of making repairs versus selling the property "as-is." Factors like the estate's financial resources, the property's market potential, and buyer expectations play a role in determining the most practical approach.

Assessing the Property's Market Value in Current Condition

Executors should begin by determining the property's market value in its current condition. A Comparative Market Analysis (CMA) from a real estate professional can provide insight into the property's potential value "as-is" versus after certain repairs. This analysis helps executors understand the realistic sale price and the potential return on any improvements.

Prioritizing Essential Repairs

If the executor decides to make improvements, it's generally wise to focus on essential repairs that address safety, structural integrity, and curb appeal. Examples might include fixing broken windows, addressing roof leaks, or repairing damaged flooring. Basic updates that enhance buyer confidence without overextending the estate's funds can improve marketability without committing to extensive renovations.

Considering the Benefits of an "As-Is" Sale

In some cases, selling the property "as-is" may be the most efficient solution, especially if the property requires extensive repairs or if the estate lacks sufficient funds. An "as-is" sale transfers the responsibility for repairs to the buyer, potentially attracting investors or buyers seeking fixer-upper opportunities. This approach minimizes the estate's expenses, allowing the probate process to move forward without delay.

Managing Additional Costs and Liabilities

Maintaining a vacant or distressed property can incur additional expenses, including utility payments, insurance premiums, and routine maintenance costs. Executors must manage these costs while balancing the estate's resources and keeping beneficiaries informed of necessary expenses.

Paying for Vacant Property Insurance

Standard homeowner's insurance may not cover vacant properties for extended periods, leaving them at risk for incidents such as vandalism, fire, or water damage. Executors should consult with the estate's insurance provider to arrange vacant property insurance, which offers additional coverage tailored to unoccupied homes. While this insurance may increase costs, it protects the estate from substantial financial loss if an incident occurs.

Budgeting for Utilities and Maintenance

Keeping essential utilities, such as electricity, water, and heating, on is important to protect the property from damage, particularly during winter months. Executors should create a budget that includes utility and maintenance costs, as well as any periodic services like landscaping or inspections. By planning ahead, executors can ensure that the property remains in good condition without overspending estate funds.

Documenting All Expenses for Court Review

Executors should keep detailed records of all maintenance-related expenses, including insurance payments, utility bills, and repair costs. These records are critical for probate court reviews and ensure that all financial actions taken were necessary for protecting the property and the estate's value.

Communicating with Beneficiaries About Property Decisions

Decisions about vacant or distressed properties can affect the estate's financial resources and distribution timelines, so it's essential for executors to keep beneficiaries informed. Transparency around the costs, risks, and potential sale options can help prevent misunderstandings and ensure that all parties understand the reasoning behind each decision.

Explaining the Condition and Cost Implications

Executors should provide beneficiaries with an overview of the property's condition, necessary expenses, and the potential impact on the estate's value. If repairs are needed to prepare the property for sale, explaining these costs helps beneficiaries understand how they support the overall estate's objectives and why they're necessary for maximizing value.

Discussing Options for "As-Is" vs. Repaired Sales

When deciding between an "as-is" sale or making repairs, executors can benefit from discussing these options with beneficiaries. Transparency around the potential costs and returns from each approach allows beneficiaries to feel involved in the decision-making process and reduces the risk of future disputes.

Final Thoughts: Managing Vacant or Distressed Properties with Care

Handling a vacant or distressed property in probate involves a unique set of responsibilities, from securing and maintaining the property to deciding whether repairs or an "as-is" sale best serves the estate. By taking steps to protect the property, budget for necessary expenses, and communicate transparently with beneficiaries, executors can preserve the estate's value and minimize potential risks. When managing complex decisions, such as whether to repair or sell "as-is," a Certified Real Estate Probate Specialist (C.P.R.S.) or probate attorney can offer valuable guidance, helping executors navigate these challenges effectively and ensure the best possible outcome for the estate.

Summary

In Chapter 7, we explored the unique challenges executors may face when managing probate properties with complex financial or physical conditions. Here are the key takeaways from each section:

1. **Managing Heir Disputes and Conflicts**: Executors often encounter differing opinions among heirs regarding the property's future. By remaining impartial, facilitating open communication, and seeking professional mediation when necessary, executors can help resolve conflicts and maintain focus on fulfilling the decedent's wishes while minimizing delays in the probate process.

2. **Properties with Outstanding Mortgages**: When a property has an outstanding mortgage, executors must ensure payments are maintained to avoid foreclosure. Options include continuing monthly payments, paying off the mortgage with estate funds, refinancing in an heir's name, or selling the property to settle the debt. Clear communication with heirs about these options can help manage expectations and maintain transparency.

3. **Dealing with Liens and Judgments**: Liens and judgments attached to probate properties must be addressed before the property can be sold or transferred. Executors should conduct a title search to identify encumbrances, prioritize and resolve liens according to Illinois law, and explore payment options, including settlements. Detailed documentation of all payments and communications is essential for court review and beneficiary transparency.

4. **Vacant or Distressed Properties**: Vacant or neglected properties require additional care to protect them from damage and maintain value. Executors should secure the property, arrange regular maintenance, and decide whether an "as-is" sale or minor repairs are most practical. Clear communication with beneficiaries about associated costs and sale options ensures transparency and reduces potential conflicts.

In summary, Chapter 7 highlighted the importance of organization, communication, and strategic decision-making when handling special situations in probate real estate. Executors can manage these challenges more effectively by staying transparent with beneficiaries, documenting all actions for court review, and seeking guidance from professionals, such as a Certified Real Estate Probate Specialist (C.P.R.S.) or probate attorney, to protect the estate's interests and facilitate a smooth probate process.

Checklist: Key Steps for Handling Special Situations in Probate Real Estate

1. Managing Heir Disputes and Conflicts
- ☐ Hold open discussions with all heirs and beneficiaries to clarify each person's expectations regarding the property and to try to reach an agreement.
- ☐ Document each family member's concerns or preferences, and aim to find common ground to avoid unnecessary delays or conflicts.
- ☐ Consider consulting a mediator or probate attorney if family disputes over the property become contentious, as professional guidance can help resolve disagreements fairly.
- ☐ Keep clear records of any decisions made and agreements reached to avoid future misunderstandings.

2. Handling Properties with Outstanding Mortgages
- ☐ Determine the status of the mortgage, including the remaining balance, monthly payment amounts, and whether payments are current.
- ☐ Review options for managing the mortgage, such as continuing payments from the estate, refinancing in an heir's name, or selling the property to pay off the mortgage.
- ☐ Contact the mortgage lender to notify them of the decedent's passing and understand any specific requirements they may have for probate properties.
- ☐ Ensure mortgage payments are made on time during probate to avoid penalties or foreclosure, particularly if the property is to be held by the estate for an extended period.

3. Dealing with Liens and Judgments
- ☐ Conduct a title search to identify any liens, judgments, or encumbrances on the property that must be addressed before it can be sold or transferred.
- ☐ Prioritize paying off liens and judgments according to Illinois probate law, using estate funds to satisfy these debts where possible.
- ☐ Consider negotiating with lienholders if funds are limited, as some creditors may agree to a settlement for less than the full amount owed.

☐ Keep thorough documentation of all lien payments and settlements, as the probate court will require proof that these debts were resolved properly.

4. Addressing Vacant or Distressed Properties

☐ Secure the property by changing locks, setting up a security system if necessary, and notifying local law enforcement that the property is temporarily vacant.

☐ Arrange for regular maintenance, such as lawn care, snow removal, and general upkeep, to preserve the property's value and comply with local codes.

☐ Evaluate the condition of the property and decide if it should be sold "as-is" or if minor repairs should be made to increase its appeal to buyers.

☐ Consider hiring a property preservation service for regular check-ins and upkeep, especially if the probate process is expected to take several months.

Chapter 8

Closing the Sale and Settling the Estate

After the probate sale is complete and the estate's obligations have been met, the final step is to officially settle the estate. This chapter covers the closing process, from paying off debts and completing tax filings to distributing assets and filing the final paperwork with the court. In Illinois, proper documentation and court filings are essential for wrapping up probate, as they confirm that all duties have been fulfilled. By following these steps, executors can ensure a smooth closing, providing closure for both the estate and the beneficiaries.

Closing the Sale of Probate Property

Once an offer on the probate property has been accepted and court confirmation (if required) is obtained, the next step is to proceed with closing the sale. The closing process for probate real estate involves additional layers of documentation and compliance compared to a standard sale, as executors must ensure that the transaction aligns with Illinois probate requirements and properly benefits the estate. Completing the closing process accurately is essential for a smooth transition of ownership and for safeguarding the estate's financial interests.

This section provides a step-by-step guide to closing the sale of a probate property, detailing key actions executors must take to finalize the transaction while maintaining transparency and compliance with Illinois probate law.

Preparing for the Closing Process

Closing a probate property sale involves several preparatory steps to ensure that all legal, financial, and property-related obligations are met. Executors should be prepared with the necessary documents and coordinate with relevant parties, including the buyer, real estate agent, attorney, and title company.

Gathering Required Documentation

Executors will need to provide a range of documents to complete the closing. These typically include the property's title, accepted purchase agreement, disclosure documents, and any additional paperwork required by the probate court. Having these documents ready in advance helps avoid delays and ensures a smooth transition through the closing process.

Verifying Clear Title Status

Ensuring that the title is free of liens, judgments, or unresolved debts is essential before closing. A title search will reveal any encumbrances that must be cleared before transferring ownership. If outstanding liens or judgments exist, they must be addressed—either through payment from sale proceeds or by reaching a settlement with creditors—before the title can be transferred to the buyer.

Communicating with the Buyer's Team

Effective communication with the buyer's agent and title company ensures all parties are aligned on the closing timeline and any final requirements. If specific conditions were agreed upon in the contract (such as repairs or concessions), the executor should confirm that these terms are fulfilled, so the buyer is prepared to proceed without issues.

Working with a Title Company for Closing

The title company plays a critical role in the closing process, managing tasks like finalizing the title transfer, coordinating the escrow account, and disbursing funds. Executors should work closely with the title company to complete each step accurately.

Confirming the Escrow Account Setup

An escrow account holds all funds associated with the sale, including the buyer's payment and any other necessary disbursements, until the transaction is complete. The title company will typically set up the escrow account and manage funds distribution according to the closing agreement. Executors should ensure the funds are held securely and accessible for disbursement to settle estate obligations.

Reviewing the Closing Disclosure Statement

The title company will prepare a closing disclosure statement that outlines all financial aspects of the sale, including the sale price, taxes, fees, and any adjustments or credits. Executors should review this document carefully to confirm accuracy, as any discrepancies can affect the final amount available to the estate. This review also ensures that all obligations, such as outstanding property taxes or transaction fees, are accounted for.

Ensuring Proper Recording of the Title Transfer

After closing, the title company will record the transfer of ownership with the county, officially finalizing the sale. Executors should confirm that the title is transferred correctly and that a copy of the recorded deed is obtained for the estate's records. This step is essential to documenting that the property was legally sold and transferred in compliance with Illinois probate law.

Disbursing Sale Proceeds to Cover Estate Obligations

Once the sale is complete and funds are available, the executor must prioritize paying any outstanding debts associated with the estate, including liens, remaining mortgage balances, property taxes, and other sale-related expenses. Only after these debts are satisfied can the net proceeds be added to the estate's assets for eventual distribution to beneficiaries.

Paying Off Mortgage and Lien Obligations

If the property had an outstanding mortgage or liens, these debts are typically paid directly from the sale proceeds at closing. Executors should confirm with the title company that all outstanding balances are fully settled before any remaining funds are released to the estate.

Covering Closing Costs and Property Taxes

The sale proceeds will also cover any closing costs, such as title insurance, transfer taxes, recording fees, and real estate agent commissions. Additionally, property taxes for the year (if not already paid) must be settled at closing, ensuring that the estate has no remaining tax obligations tied to the property.

Allocating Net Proceeds to the Estate

After all debts, fees, and taxes are covered, the remaining funds—referred to as net proceeds—are transferred to the estate account. These proceeds are then available for use in satisfying other estate debts, expenses, and, ultimately, distribution to beneficiaries according to the decedent's will or Illinois intestacy laws.

Documenting the Closing Process for the Court and Beneficiaries

Transparency and documentation are essential during closing, as executors will need to demonstrate to the probate court and beneficiaries that the sale was completed in compliance with probate law and that all funds were managed responsibly.

Keeping Detailed Financial Records

Executors should maintain thorough records of all financial transactions associated with the sale, including copies of the final purchase agreement, closing disclosure statement, title transfer documents, and receipts for any disbursements made to creditors or the estate. These records provide a comprehensive account of how the property sale was managed and ensure transparency for all parties involved.

Preparing a Final Report for the Court

In Illinois, probate courts often require a detailed report outlining the sale, proceeds allocation, and how remaining funds were added to the estate. Executors should prepare a summary of the transaction, including a breakdown of how funds were used to settle debts and any remaining balance for distribution. Working with a probate attorney may simplify this reporting process and help ensure compliance with Illinois probate requirements.

Communicating with Beneficiaries

After closing, executors should update beneficiaries about the sale's completion and provide an overview of how the net proceeds will be allocated within the estate. Clear communication helps prevent misunderstandings and keeps beneficiaries informed of the estate's progress toward final distribution.

Final Thoughts: Completing the Probate Property Sale with Care and Accuracy

The closing process for a probate property sale is a critical step that involves careful coordination and attention to detail. By preparing necessary documents, working closely with the title company, and ensuring all debts and expenses are settled, executors can finalize the sale smoothly. Clear documentation and communication with the court and beneficiaries provide transparency and demonstrate the executor's commitment to fulfilling their fiduciary duties. This step ultimately prepares the estate for the next stages of settling debts, filing final taxes, and distributing assets to heirs, allowing the probate process to proceed toward closure.

Paying Off Debts and Distributing Assets

Once the probate property sale is complete and the proceeds have been added to the estate, the executor's next responsibility is to pay off any outstanding debts before distributing remaining assets to beneficiaries. Illinois probate law requires that estate debts be settled in a specific order of priority, ensuring that all legitimate claims against the estate are addressed. By managing these obligations transparently and keeping beneficiaries informed, executors can fulfill their fiduciary duty and lay the groundwork for a smooth asset distribution.

This section outlines the key steps executors must take to prioritize, pay off, and document estate debts, as well as how to prepare for final asset distribution in accordance with Illinois probate requirements.

Identifying and Prioritizing Estate Debts

The first step in settling the estate is to identify all outstanding debts and prioritize them according to Illinois probate law. Certain debts, such as funeral expenses and taxes, take precedence and must be paid before other claims. Executors should carefully review each claim to ensure they meet legal obligations while protecting the estate's assets for beneficiaries.

Reviewing Creditor Claims and Debts

Executors should collect all claims submitted by creditors, as well as any outstanding bills or known debts. Common debts include medical bills, credit card balances, utility bills, and loans. If creditors have submitted claims, the executor must review and verify each one to ensure it's legitimate and aligns with the estate's financial records.

Following Illinois Priority of Payments

Under Illinois law, estate debts are prioritized as follows:

- Funeral and burial expenses

- Administrative costs (e.g., executor fees, legal fees)

- Medical expenses from the decedent's last illness

- Family allowances (if applicable)

- Other debts, such as taxes and secured loans

Executors should follow this order when paying debts, as failing to do so could result in legal issues or delays. If funds are limited, prioritizing debts ensures that the estate's most essential obligations are met first.

Paying Off Debts Using Estate Assets

Once debts are identified and prioritized, executors can begin paying them using estate funds. This may involve liquidating other assets or using proceeds from the property sale to satisfy all obligations. Executors should keep clear records of each payment, including receipts and transaction details, to provide a transparent account of how estate funds were used.

Using Liquid Assets for Payment

If the estate has liquid assets, such as cash accounts, these funds can be used directly to pay off debts. This approach simplifies the process, as liquid assets are readily available and don't require additional transactions or liquidation efforts. Executors should ensure all payments are properly recorded in the estate's financial records.

Selling or Liquidating Non-Liquid Assets

In cases where liquid assets are insufficient, the executor may need to liquidate other estate assets, such as stocks, bonds, or valuable personal property. Executors should consider the implications of liquidating certain assets and aim to preserve as much value as possible for beneficiaries. Working with a financial advisor or probate attorney may help identify the most effective approach for asset liquidation.

Settling Secured Debts with Sale Proceeds

Secured debts, such as mortgages or liens tied to the property, are typically paid directly from the sale proceeds during closing. Executors should confirm with the title company that all secured debts were fully settled from the sale funds and ensure any remaining debt obligations are resolved before moving on to asset distribution.

Documenting All Payments and Settlements

Accurate documentation of each debt payment is critical for the executor's final accounting and for court review. Executors should maintain organized records of all transactions, including receipts, bank statements, and settlement letters, as these documents provide evidence that estate funds were used responsibly and in compliance with Illinois law.

Maintaining Detailed Financial Records

Executors should record each payment, including the date, amount, payee, and purpose of the transaction. This level of detail is important for probate court records and reassures beneficiaries that the executor fulfilled their fiduciary duty in managing estate funds.

Preparing for Final Accounting to the Court

In Illinois, probate courts typically require a final accounting that details how estate funds were allocated, including debt payments. Executors should compile a comprehensive financial report that outlines all transactions, from initial asset inventory to final debt settlements, providing full transparency of the estate's financial management.

Communicating with Beneficiaries During the Debt Settlement Process

Executors should keep beneficiaries informed throughout the debt settlement process, especially if significant portions of the estate's assets are needed to cover debts. Clear communication can help manage expectations and prevent misunderstandings about the amount remaining for distribution.

Providing Updates on Estate Expenses

Executors should notify beneficiaries about major expenses, including funeral costs, administrative fees, and any unexpected debts. Transparency in communicating these expenses helps beneficiaries understand how much of the estate's assets were required to settle debts and may reduce the likelihood of disputes.

Setting Expectations for Asset Distribution

If the estate's debts consume a large portion of its assets, executors should be upfront with beneficiaries about the potential impact on their inheritance. Having realistic expectations allows beneficiaries to prepare for the final distribution and minimizes potential disappointments.

Preparing for Asset Distribution After Debt Settlement

Once all debts and obligations are cleared, the executor can prepare for asset distribution. At this stage, the executor will allocate remaining assets to beneficiaries according to the decedent's will or, if no will exists, in accordance with Illinois intestacy laws. Proper documentation and adherence to probate requirements ensure that the distribution process goes smoothly and complies with legal obligations.

Reviewing the Will or Illinois Intestacy Laws

The executor should refer to the decedent's will to determine each beneficiary's share of the remaining assets. If the decedent passed away without a will, Illinois intestacy laws provide a specific order of distribution based on familial relationships. Executors should be prepared to follow these guidelines carefully to ensure all beneficiaries receive their lawful share.

Preparing Transfer Documents for Beneficiaries

For assets such as real estate, investment accounts, or valuable personal property, executors may need to prepare transfer documents to legally assign ownership to beneficiaries. Working with a probate attorney or financial advisor can help executors handle complex asset transfers and complete all necessary paperwork accurately.

Final Thoughts: Paying Off Debts and Preparing for Distribution

Settling an estate's debts is a critical responsibility for executors, ensuring that all obligations are met before distributing assets to beneficiaries. By prioritizing debts according to Illinois law, maintaining detailed records, and communicating with beneficiaries, executors fulfill their fiduciary duties and create a clear path for asset distribution. As executors move forward, following these steps not only protects the estate's value but also provides transparency to the court and beneficiaries, paving the way for final tax filings, court documents, and the eventual closing of probate.

Completing Final Tax Filings

Before the probate estate can be officially closed, executors must ensure that all required tax filings are completed. This includes both federal and Illinois state tax obligations, such as the decedent's final income tax return, any estate income tax filings, and potential estate tax filings if the estate meets certain value thresholds. Addressing these tax requirements is essential to avoid potential penalties, settle all outstanding liabilities, and finalize the distribution of assets to beneficiaries.

This section provides a guide to the types of tax filings required in probate, how to prepare them, and strategies for managing complex tax situations that may arise.

Filing the Decedent's Final Income Tax Return

The decedent's final personal income tax return (Form 1040) must be filed for the year in which they passed away. This return reports all income earned up to the date of death and is due on the standard tax filing deadline of April 15 the following year. Executors are responsible for gathering the decedent's financial records, preparing the return, and ensuring that any outstanding tax liability is paid from the estate's assets.

Gathering Financial Records and Documents

To prepare the decedent's final income tax return, executors must collect relevant financial records, such as W-2s, 1099 forms, and other income documentation. Executors should also locate records of deductible expenses, including medical expenses, mortgage interest, or charitable contributions made by the decedent during their final year.

Filing State Income Taxes

In addition to the federal return, executors must file a state income tax return for Illinois if the decedent was a resident or earned income in

Illinois. The requirements and deadlines for state income taxes mirror the federal return, so executors should ensure both returns are filed by the April 15 deadline unless an extension is requested.

Seeking Professional Tax Assistance if Needed

If the decedent's financial situation is complex—such as if they had multiple income sources or significant deductions—executors may benefit from working with a tax professional to prepare the return accurately. A certified tax preparer or CPA can ensure that all income and deductions are properly reported, minimizing the risk of errors or missed tax credits.

Filing the Estate Income Tax Return (Form 1041)

If the estate generates income during the probate process (e.g., from investments, rental income, or the sale of estate assets), the executor must file an estate income tax return (Form 1041) on behalf of the estate. This return reports any income earned after the decedent's death and is separate from the decedent's personal income tax return.

Determining if the Estate Earned Taxable Income

Executors should evaluate whether the estate generated any income during probate. Common sources of estate income include interest, dividends, rental payments, or capital gains from the sale of assets. If the estate earns $600 or more in income in a given year, a Form 1041 is required to report this income to the IRS.

Reporting Expenses and Deductions

Certain expenses paid during probate—such as administrative costs, legal fees, and property maintenance expenses—may be deductible on the estate's income tax return. Executors should keep detailed records of these expenses, as they can offset the estate's taxable income and potentially reduce the estate's overall tax liability.

Filing Deadlines and Extensions for Form 1041

The estate income tax return is typically due on April 15 of the year following the income-earning year, although a fiscal year option is available if the estate prefers a different filing schedule. If the estate income tax filing cannot be completed by the deadline, executors can request an extension, providing additional time to finalize the estate's financial activities and report income accurately.

Assessing Estate Tax Obligations

While federal estate taxes apply only to estates with values above a certain threshold ($12.92 million as of 2023), Illinois imposes its own estate tax on estates valued over $4 million. Executors must assess whether the estate's total value exceeds these limits, which would require filing a separate estate tax return and possibly paying taxes owed from the estate's assets.

Determining the Estate's Total Value

The estate's value includes all assets owned by the decedent at the time of death, such as real estate, bank accounts, investments, retirement accounts, and personal property. Executors should complete a thorough inventory of assets and calculate the total value to determine if the estate meets the Illinois or federal tax filing thresholds.

Filing an Illinois Estate Tax Return

If the estate's value exceeds $4 million, Illinois requires the filing of an estate tax return within nine months of the decedent's date of death. This return calculates the amount of estate tax owed to the state, which must be paid from the estate's assets. Executors should file the Illinois estate tax return in compliance with state guidelines to avoid penalties and protect the estate from potential legal issues.

Filing a Federal Estate Tax Return (Form 706), If Required

For estates exceeding the federal threshold, Form 706 must be filed with the IRS within nine months of the decedent's death. This form calculates the federal estate tax owed, if any, and documents the estate's full financial picture. Given the complexity of federal estate tax filings, executors should consider working with an estate attorney or tax professional if Form 706 is required, as accurate reporting is essential to avoid costly penalties.

Managing Final Tax Payments from the Estate

If taxes are owed, the executor is responsible for ensuring they are paid from the estate's funds. Paying taxes promptly from estate assets is critical, as delays or missed payments can lead to penalties and interest that impact the estate's value. Executors should confirm that funds are available to cover these liabilities and, if necessary, consider selling assets to generate the needed liquidity.

Using Estate Assets for Tax Payments

Executors can use estate accounts or liquidate other assets, if necessary, to pay any outstanding tax liabilities. Ensuring these payments are made in full and on time is important for maintaining compliance and protecting the estate's financial integrity.

Documenting All Tax Payments

Clear records of all tax payments should be maintained as part of the estate's financial documentation. This includes keeping copies of filed tax returns, receipts of payment, and any correspondence with tax authorities. These records are necessary for the final accounting and to demonstrate to the court and beneficiaries that the estate's tax obligations were met fully and accurately.

Communicating with Beneficiaries About Tax Implications

Since tax payments affect the overall distribution of assets, executors should communicate with beneficiaries regarding any tax liabilities and how they impact the estate. This transparency helps beneficiaries understand the necessary deductions from the estate's assets and prevents misunderstandings about the final distribution amounts.

Providing Beneficiaries with Estimated Distributions

Executors can share estimated distribution amounts with beneficiaries, taking tax obligations into account. This helps set realistic expectations about the funds or assets each beneficiary will receive, ensuring that any potential reductions due to tax payments are understood.

Preparing for K-1 Forms for Beneficiaries

If the estate generated income that passed through to beneficiaries, executors may need to provide each beneficiary with a Schedule K-1 from Form 1041. The K-1 details each beneficiary's share of the estate's income, which they must report on their personal income tax returns. Preparing these forms and sharing them with beneficiaries ensures compliance and prepares beneficiaries for their own tax responsibilities.

Final Thoughts: Completing Tax Filings as a Key Step in Closing Probate

Completing all necessary tax filings is an essential step in the probate process, ensuring that the estate meets both state and federal obligations before distributing assets to beneficiaries. By filing the decedent's final income tax return, assessing estate income tax requirements, and managing estate taxes as needed, executors can prevent legal and financial complications that might otherwise delay probate closure. Clear documentation and communication with beneficiaries allow executors to fulfill their fiduciary duties and keep the estate on track for final court filings and closure.

Final Court Filings and Closing Probate

Once all debts have been paid, taxes filed, and assets prepared for distribution, the final step in probate is to complete the necessary court filings to officially close the estate. In Illinois, the probate court requires a final accounting and detailed records of all estate activities to confirm that the executor has fulfilled their fiduciary duties. By filing this documentation, obtaining the court's approval, and securing final closure, executors conclude their responsibilities, allowing assets to be distributed to beneficiaries and officially ending the probate process.

This section covers the key steps in filing the final paperwork, ensuring compliance with Illinois probate requirements, and achieving formal closure of the estate.

Preparing the Final Accounting for the Court

The final accounting provides the probate court with a comprehensive overview of how the estate's assets were managed, including all receipts, expenses, and distributions made. This report is critical for ensuring transparency and demonstrating that the executor acted responsibly and in the best interests of the estate and its beneficiaries.

Documenting All Financial Transactions

Executors must compile a thorough record of all financial transactions that occurred during probate. This includes details on funds received, property sales, debt payments, tax payments, and any expenses paid on behalf of the estate. Accurate documentation allows the court to verify the executor's actions and confirm that funds were handled appropriately.

Organizing Receipts and Supporting Documents

In addition to financial records, executors should organize receipts, invoices, and other supporting documents that substantiate each transaction. These records provide concrete evidence of all expenses and payments, making the final accounting as complete and transparent as possible. By presenting a well-organized report, executors demonstrate their commitment to fulfilling their fiduciary duties.

Reviewing the Accounting with a Probate Attorney

To ensure accuracy and compliance, many executors benefit from reviewing the final accounting with a probate attorney. An attorney can help identify any potential gaps or areas requiring clarification, ensuring the report meets Illinois probate standards and minimizing the likelihood of court objections or delays.

Submitting the Final Accounting and Petition for Distribution

Once the final accounting is complete, the executor must file it with the probate court, along with a petition for distribution. This petition requests court approval to distribute the remaining assets to beneficiaries, signaling the last step before the estate can be officially closed.

Filing the Petition and Notifying Beneficiaries

After filing the final accounting and petition for distribution, the executor must notify beneficiaries and provide them with copies of the documents. Beneficiaries have the right to review the final accounting and may raise any questions or objections. Clear communication with beneficiaries about the contents of the final accounting can help preemptively address concerns and prevent misunderstandings.

Attending the Final Court Hearing

The probate court will schedule a final hearing to review the accounting and consider any beneficiary objections. If the court is satisfied with the documentation and finds that the executor acted appropriately, it will grant approval for distribution. Executors should be prepared to answer questions about their management of the estate and to clarify any aspects of the final accounting if requested by the court.

Resolving Any Objections

If beneficiaries raise objections to the final accounting, the court may require additional documentation or revisions before granting approval. Executors should work with a probate attorney to resolve any disputes efficiently, as addressing objections promptly ensures that the estate closure process remains on track.

Distributing Assets to Beneficiaries

Once the court approves the final accounting and distribution plan, the executor can proceed with distributing the remaining assets to beneficiaries. This final step involves transferring ownership of each asset according to the decedent's will or, if there is no will, Illinois intestacy laws.

Executing Transfers of Property and Funds

For liquid assets, such as cash accounts, executors can distribute funds directly to beneficiaries. For other assets, such as real estate, vehicles, or valuable personal property, the executor must prepare transfer documents to assign ownership legally. Working with a probate attorney may simplify complex asset transfers and ensure they meet legal requirements.

Providing Beneficiaries with Distribution Statements

It's advisable for executors to prepare distribution statements for each beneficiary, outlining the assets or funds they received and how the value was calculated. These statements provide transparency and create a clear record of how the estate's assets were distributed, helping to prevent misunderstandings or disputes after probate closure.

Securing Acknowledgment of Receipt from Beneficiaries

To finalize the distribution, executors may request that beneficiaries sign an acknowledgment of receipt for the assets or funds they received. This signed statement confirms that beneficiaries have received their inheritance in full, protecting the executor from future claims and documenting the completion of asset distribution.

Obtaining a Final Discharge and Closing Probate

The final step in the probate process is obtaining a discharge from the court, which officially releases the executor from their duties. This discharge signals that all estate matters have been resolved in compliance with Illinois law, allowing probate to be formally closed.

Filing a Petition for Discharge

After distributions are complete, the executor must file a petition for discharge with the probate court. This petition requests a formal release from responsibilities, affirming that all duties have been fulfilled and that the estate has been settled in accordance with the court's instructions.

Receiving the Court's Order for Final Discharge

Once the court reviews the petition and confirms that all requirements have been met, it will issue an order for final discharge. This court order provides official closure of the probate estate, releasing the executor from further obligations. Executors should retain a copy of this discharge order for their records as it serves as proof of probate completion.

Informing Beneficiaries of Probate Closure

After receiving the final discharge, executors should inform beneficiaries that probate is officially closed. This communication brings closure to the beneficiaries as well, marking the conclusion of the probate process and confirming that all estate matters have been handled responsibly.

Final Thoughts: Successfully Concluding the Probate Process

Completing the final court filings and securing closure of probate is the culmination of an executor's responsibilities. By preparing an accurate final accounting, obtaining court approval for asset distribution, and securing a discharge, executors fulfill their fiduciary duty and bring the estate's probate process to a formal end. This final step not only provides closure for beneficiaries but also ensures that the estate has been settled in full compliance with Illinois probate law. With probate now closed, beneficiaries can move forward with their inheritance, and executors can take satisfaction in having successfully managed the estate with care and integrity.

Summary

In Chapter 8, we covered the essential steps to conclude probate and settle the estate. This chapter focused on wrapping up financial, legal, and court requirements, ensuring executors fulfill their responsibilities in compliance with Illinois probate law. Here are the key takeaways:

1. **Closing the Sale of Probate Property**: Executors finalized the sale by gathering required documents, working with a title company, and confirming that sale proceeds were used to settle any remaining property-related debts. Keeping accurate records ensured that the sale was fully compliant and ready for court review.

2. **Paying Off Debts and Distributing Assets**: Before distribution, executors prioritized and paid the estate's outstanding debts according to Illinois probate guidelines. Clear documentation of all payments, along with communication with beneficiaries, ensured that these obligations were settled transparently and in the estate's best interest.

3. **Completing Final Tax Filings**: Executors completed necessary tax filings, including the decedent's final income tax return, any estate income tax filings, and potential estate tax returns for Illinois or federal purposes. Addressing tax obligations carefully prevented penalties and delays, protecting the estate's remaining assets.

4. **Final Court Filings and Closing Probate**: The last step involved submitting a final accounting to the court, gaining approval for distributions, and obtaining a discharge to formally close probate. By providing detailed financial records and clear communication with beneficiaries, executors demonstrated that they had acted in compliance with their fiduciary duty and completed all probate responsibilities.

In summary, Chapter 8 highlighted the importance of accuracy, documentation, and communication in the final stages of probate. By addressing each obligation methodically, executors can confidently bring the probate process to a close, ensuring a transparent transition of assets to beneficiaries and fulfilling their legal responsibilities.

Checklist: Key Steps for Closing the Sale and Settling the Estate

1. Closing the Sale of Probate Property

☐ Ensure all necessary documents for the property sale are completed and submitted, including the closing disclosure, purchase agreement, and any required probate court filings.

☐ Confirm that any conditions or contingencies in the buyer's offer are met and documented to prevent delays in the closing process.

☐ Verify that the title company has recorded the title transfer and that all sale proceeds are securely held in an estate account for distribution.

☐ Keep detailed records of the closing process, including any payments made to cover final fees, property taxes, and mortgage or lien payoffs.

2. Paying Off Debts and Distributing Assets

☐ Create a list of all outstanding debts, including mortgages, liens, taxes, medical bills, and credit card balances, and ensure they are prioritized according to Illinois probate law.

☐ Pay off all debts in the correct order of priority, starting with probate and administration costs, funeral expenses, and other obligations, ensuring compliance with Illinois statutes.

☐ Record each payment with details on the date, amount, and payee, and keep receipts and transaction records for court reporting and beneficiary transparency.

☐ After debts are paid, prepare for asset distribution by confirming the remaining assets in the estate account and ensuring they align with the terms of the will or Illinois intestacy laws.

3. Completing Final Tax Filings

☐ File the decedent's final personal income tax return (Form 1040) for the year of their passing, ensuring all income is accurately reported and taxes are paid.

☐ Complete an estate income tax return (Form 1041) if the estate earned income during the probate process, such as interest or rental income.

☐ Determine if Illinois or federal estate tax filings are required by assessing the estate's total value and consulting with a tax professional if needed.

☐ Keep copies of all tax filings, payment receipts, and relevant documentation, as these records may be required for final court review and beneficiary information.

4. Final Court Filings and Closing Probate

☐ Prepare a final accounting report that summarizes all estate transactions, including asset sales, debt payments, distributions, and administrative expenses.

☐ File a petition for distribution and final accounting with the probate court, requesting approval to distribute assets to beneficiaries.

☐ Notify beneficiaries of the court hearing date for the final accounting, giving them an opportunity to review the report and raise any questions.

☐ Obtain the court's approval for final distribution and a discharge order, officially releasing the executor from further responsibilities and closing the probate case.

☐ Inform beneficiaries that the estate is now closed, and provide any necessary distribution statements or documents for their records.

Chapter 9

Alternatives to Probate for Future Planning

While probate is a necessary process for many, there are ways to simplify estate planning to reduce or even avoid probate altogether. In this final chapter, we'll explore probate-free transfer options, including living trusts, joint tenancy, and beneficiary deeds. We'll also discuss the importance of creating a comprehensive estate plan that incorporates these tools to provide peace of mind for you and your family. By considering these alternatives, you can create a plan that streamlines inheritance, preserves privacy, and ensures your assets are managed according to your wishes, all while easing the process for your loved ones.

Trusts as a Probate Alternative

For those looking to minimize the complexities of probate, creating a trust can be one of the most effective solutions. A trust allows assets to bypass probate entirely, which can save time, reduce costs, and provide greater privacy for families. Trusts are especially valuable in Illinois, where the probate process can take months and often requires public disclosure of estate assets. A properly structured living trust not only protects a person's assets during their lifetime but also ensures a smoother transfer of those assets to beneficiaries after their death.

This section explores how trusts work, their benefits as an alternative to probate, and why establishing a trust could be a wise choice for future estate planning.

Understanding Living Trusts as a Probate-Free Tool

A living trust, also known as a revocable trust, is a legal entity created to hold and manage assets. During a person's lifetime, they can place their property, bank accounts, investments, and other assets into the trust while retaining control over them as the "trustee." Upon their death, the trust's assets are distributed directly to designated beneficiaries by a successor trustee, bypassing the probate court altogether.

Revocable vs. Irrevocable Trusts

Living trusts are typically "revocable," meaning that the creator, or grantor, can change or dissolve the trust at any time during their lifetime. This flexibility makes revocable trusts a popular option for those looking to maintain control of their assets while preparing for the future. On the other hand, "irrevocable" trusts, which generally cannot be altered once established, offer additional tax and asset protection benefits but are less commonly used as probate-avoidance tools.

Role of the Trustee and Successor Trustee

The trustee is responsible for managing and overseeing the assets within the trust, and in a living trust, this is usually the person who created it. They retain full control over the trust's assets, just as they would if they owned them outright. The successor trustee, who is appointed in advance, steps in to manage and distribute the assets according to the trust's terms upon the grantor's death, ensuring that the estate transfers smoothly to beneficiaries without court involvement.

Advantages of Using a Living Trust to Avoid Probate

Bypassing probate is one of the primary benefits of creating a living trust. Avoiding probate can reduce costs, protect privacy, and expedite the distribution of assets to beneficiaries, making trusts an attractive option for those looking to streamline the estate settlement process for their loved ones.

Faster Access to Assets for Beneficiaries

One of the major benefits of a living trust is that it allows beneficiaries to access assets more quickly than they would through probate. Probate can take months or even years, whereas assets held in a trust are distributed almost immediately after the grantor's death. This is especially helpful if beneficiaries rely on these assets to cover immediate expenses, such as funeral costs, or to continue operating family businesses.

Privacy and Confidentiality

Unlike probate, which is a public process in Illinois, trusts allow for a private transfer of assets. Probate records are accessible to the public, meaning details about the estate's assets and beneficiaries are visible to anyone interested. With a trust, however, asset transfers and beneficiary designations remain confidential, providing families with an extra layer of privacy.

Reduced Costs and Simplified Administration

While establishing a trust involves upfront legal costs, the expense is often balanced out by the money saved on probate fees and court costs. Because the trust bypasses probate, families can avoid expenses associated with probate filings, appraisals, and potential attorney fees, simplifying the overall administration of the estate.

Additional Benefits of Trusts in Estate Planning

Beyond bypassing probate, living trusts offer additional benefits that can enhance estate planning by addressing unique family needs and providing flexibility in asset management. A living trust can protect assets for beneficiaries, particularly if they are minors or individuals who may not be equipped to manage significant inheritances.

Asset Protection for Beneficiaries

Living trusts can include provisions that protect beneficiaries who may need guidance in managing their inheritance. For example, the trust can be structured to distribute funds gradually, rather than as a lump sum, ensuring that younger beneficiaries or those with financial management challenges receive support over time. This controlled distribution can reduce the risk of mismanagement or depletion of inherited assets.

Flexibility for Changing Circumstances

A revocable trust offers flexibility for the grantor to adjust terms, beneficiaries, or assets as circumstances change. This adaptability is helpful for those who may want to add new assets to the trust, update beneficiary designations, or adjust the timing and conditions of distributions based on family dynamics.

Planning for Incapacity

In addition to addressing estate planning needs, a living trust can play a critical role in planning for incapacity. If the grantor becomes incapacitated due to illness or injury, the successor trustee can step in to manage the trust assets, ensuring bills are paid and assets are preserved. This feature can be particularly valuable for those who want to ensure their affairs are managed smoothly if they are unable to make decisions themselves.

Setting Up a Trust: What to Consider

Establishing a living trust is a relatively straightforward process, but it's essential to work with an experienced estate planning attorney to ensure the trust is legally sound and aligns with the grantor's intentions. Executors and grantors should keep several key considerations in mind when setting up a trust.

Selecting a Knowledgeable Successor Trustee

Choosing a trustworthy and capable successor trustee is essential to the success of a living trust. The successor trustee will handle the responsibility of distributing assets, managing any ongoing trust activities, and communicating with beneficiaries. Many people choose a trusted family member or a professional trustee, such as an attorney or financial institution, who is experienced in managing trusts.

Funding the Trust Properly

A trust is only effective if it is properly funded, meaning that assets are transferred into the trust during the grantor's lifetime. This includes retitling property, bank accounts, investment portfolios, and other valuable assets into the trust's name. Failing to transfer these assets into the trust could result in them going through probate, defeating the purpose of establishing a trust in the first place.

Keeping the Trust Up to Date

Just as life circumstances change, so too should an estate plan. A living trust should be reviewed periodically to ensure it reflects the grantor's current wishes, especially after major life events, such as marriage, divorce, the birth of children, or significant changes in financial status. Updating the trust keeps it aligned with the grantor's evolving family dynamics and estate planning goals.

Final Thoughts: Trusts as an Effective Tool to Avoid Probate

Living trusts offer a versatile and effective way to avoid probate while giving families greater control, privacy, and flexibility over their estate. By placing assets in a living trust, individuals can ensure a smooth transition of their property to loved ones, reducing the administrative burden and protecting their legacy. For Illinois residents, where probate can be time-consuming and public, creating a living trust is an option well worth considering. For assistance in setting up a trust tailored to individual needs, consulting with an experienced estate planning attorney can provide valuable guidance and peace of mind.

Joint Tenancy and Beneficiary Deeds

In addition to trusts, certain property arrangements and title designations allow individuals to transfer assets without going through probate. Joint tenancy and beneficiary deeds are two common methods that simplify the inheritance process by enabling a direct transfer to heirs. Both options allow assets to pass to beneficiaries more quickly and with fewer administrative requirements than probate, making them popular choices for those seeking an efficient, straightforward way to manage property transfers.

This section explores joint tenancy and beneficiary deeds, outlining their unique benefits, limitations, and the circumstances in which they might be best suited.

Joint Tenancy: Shared Ownership with Automatic Transfer

Joint tenancy is a form of property ownership in which two or more people own a property equally with "rights of survivorship." This means that when one owner (or "joint tenant") dies, their share of the property automatically passes to the surviving joint tenant(s), bypassing probate entirely. Joint tenancy is commonly used for real estate, bank accounts, and other jointly owned assets.

How Joint Tenancy Works

When property is owned in joint tenancy, each owner has an equal share, and ownership transfers directly to the remaining owner(s) upon death. For example, if two people jointly own a home, each holds a 50% interest. When one owner passes away, the surviving owner automatically receives full ownership without probate, regardless of any terms in a will.

Benefits of Joint Tenancy

Avoids Probate: The automatic transfer of ownership allows assets to bypass probate, providing immediate access to the surviving owner.

Simple and Direct: Joint tenancy is straightforward and does not require additional legal documents once the title is established.

No Additional Costs: Unlike some estate planning tools, joint tenancy typically does not require ongoing costs or legal fees beyond the initial title arrangement.

Drawbacks of Joint Tenancy

Lack of Flexibility: All joint tenants must agree on property decisions, such as selling or refinancing, limiting individual control.

No Control Over Inheritance: Because the transfer happens automatically, the deceased's share cannot be redirected to other heirs, which may cause unintended consequences.

Potential Tax Implications: Adding a non-spouse as a joint tenant can have tax implications, such as gift taxes, making it important to consult a tax professional.

Beneficiary Deeds: A Transfer-on-Death Option for Real Estate

A beneficiary deed, or transfer-on-death (TOD) deed, is another effective way to avoid probate, allowing property to pass directly to designated beneficiaries upon the owner's death. Unlike joint tenancy, a beneficiary deed does not grant current ownership rights; the transfer takes effect only after death, allowing the owner full control over the property during their lifetime.

How Beneficiary Deeds Work

A beneficiary deed names one or more beneficiaries who will inherit the property automatically when the owner dies. The deed is filed with the county recorder, and the owner retains full control to sell, refinance, or change the beneficiary designation as needed. When the owner passes away, the property transfers directly to the beneficiary without court involvement.

Benefits of Beneficiary Deeds

Maintains Owner Control: The property owner has full control to manage, sell, or alter the property or beneficiary designation while alive.

Avoids Probate: Similar to joint tenancy, the property bypasses probate, allowing a quicker, simpler transfer to beneficiaries.

Flexibility: The deed can be easily modified or revoked, giving owners freedom to update their estate plans as circumstances change.

Limitations of Beneficiary Deeds

Single-Asset Focus: Beneficiary deeds apply only to the specific property listed, requiring separate deeds for multiple properties.

Creditors' Claims: The property remains subject to any of the owner's debts or creditor claims after death, unlike some types of trusts that can shield assets.

Limited Applicability for Complex Estates: For estates with multiple properties or complicated inheritance plans, beneficiary deeds alone may not fully cover all estate planning needs.

Deciding When to Use Joint Tenancy or Beneficiary Deeds

Both joint tenancy and beneficiary deeds are useful probate-avoidance tools, but each has unique strengths depending on individual goals, family structure, and financial situation.

Joint Tenancy for Spouses and Family Members

Joint tenancy is particularly suited to spouses or close family members who share ownership of primary residences or bank accounts and want a seamless transfer upon death. However, because it limits inheritance flexibility, joint tenancy may not be ideal for individuals with more complex family dynamics or multiple heirs.

Beneficiary Deeds for Individual Control

Beneficiary deeds are an excellent option for individuals who want to retain full control over their property while ensuring a probate-free transfer. Single property owners or those with specific inheritance preferences often benefit from the flexibility of beneficiary deeds, as these can be adjusted or revoked without involving other parties.

Combining with Other Estate Planning Tools

In some cases, using joint tenancy and beneficiary deeds in combination with a trust or other estate planning options can create a well-rounded plan. For example, a primary residence might be held in joint tenancy with a spouse, while other properties are designated through beneficiary deeds or included in a trust. Working with an estate planning attorney can help tailor an approach that aligns with each person's unique circumstances and goals.

Final Thoughts: Simplifying Transfers with Joint Tenancy and Beneficiary Deeds

Joint tenancy and beneficiary deeds are effective tools for avoiding probate, offering quick and direct ways to transfer assets to heirs. By choosing the right method based on their needs, individuals can simplify the inheritance process for their loved ones while retaining control over their assets. For more complex estates or detailed inheritance goals, consulting an estate planning professional can help determine the best combination of tools to protect assets, minimize court involvement, and ensure a smooth transition for beneficiaries.

Creating an Estate Plan

While individual tools like trusts, joint tenancy, and beneficiary deeds each offer specific advantages for bypassing probate, a well-rounded estate plan goes beyond these standalone options. A comprehensive estate plan takes a holistic approach, combining probate-free transfer tools with clear instructions for managing assets, handling debts, and supporting loved ones. By creating an estate plan that reflects their wishes, individuals can provide clarity, simplify the inheritance process, and ensure that their families are cared for according to their intentions.

This section discusses the benefits of estate planning, key elements to include, and tips for building a plan that supports a smooth transition of assets while reducing the emotional and financial burdens on heirs.

The Value of Comprehensive Estate Planning

Estate planning isn't just about deciding who will inherit certain assets; it's about giving families guidance and structure that can ease decision-making during difficult times. A comprehensive plan protects assets, prevents misunderstandings, and reduces the potential for costly delays or conflicts. For many Illinois families, creating an estate plan helps ensure that loved ones avoid the common pitfalls of probate and benefit from a clear path forward.

Achieving Clarity and Control

An estate plan enables individuals to express their wishes clearly, addressing questions of inheritance, asset management, and care in the event of incapacity. With an estate plan, individuals can control how their assets will be managed and distributed, reducing the need for probate court involvement and ensuring assets reach beneficiaries in the intended way.

Reducing Stress for Family Members

An estate plan provides instructions for managing the estate, minimizing the burden on family members to make difficult decisions without guidance. Having a plan in place helps prevent family disputes, protects relationships, and gives loved ones a sense of direction.

Avoiding Probate and Associated Costs

By including probate-free tools such as living trusts, joint tenancy, and beneficiary deeds in their estate plan, individuals can avoid the delays, fees, and public disclosures associated with probate. Avoiding probate can save families considerable time and expense, preserving more of the estate's value for heirs.

Key Components of an Estate Plan

A well-rounded estate plan includes several core components that address asset distribution, legal protection, and ongoing care needs. Executors, family members, and beneficiaries benefit when these elements are thoughtfully combined to meet unique family dynamics and financial goals.

Last Will and Testament

While probate-free tools like trusts and beneficiary deeds help transfer assets outside probate, a will remains essential for addressing assets not included in these tools. A will designates an executor to oversee the estate and outlines specific inheritance instructions for personal property, business interests, or other items not covered elsewhere.

Living Trust

As discussed in previous sections, a living trust provides flexibility and control over assets while bypassing probate. It can be especially helpful for those with significant assets, real estate, or minor beneficiaries, as it allows the grantor to establish specific conditions for inheritance.

Trusts also offer privacy and streamline the distribution process for complex estates.

Power of Attorney and Healthcare Directive

Estate planning also includes preparing for potential incapacity. A durable power of attorney authorizes a trusted individual to make financial or legal decisions on the person's behalf if they become unable to do so. Similarly, a healthcare directive or living will ensures that healthcare wishes are honored if the individual is incapacitated, protecting both medical and personal choices.

Beneficiary Designations on Financial Accounts

Certain assets, like life insurance policies, retirement accounts, and bank accounts, allow the account holder to name beneficiaries directly. Ensuring beneficiary designations are accurate and up to date keeps these accounts out of probate and ensures assets transfer quickly to intended heirs. Regularly reviewing and updating these designations is essential, especially after major life changes.

Steps to Building an Effective Estate Plan

Creating an estate plan can feel overwhelming, but breaking it down into manageable steps helps streamline the process. Each estate plan should reflect the unique values, family structure, and financial goals of the individual, ensuring a thoughtful approach that minimizes stress and confusion.

Assessing Assets and Liabilities

The first step in building an estate plan is to create a detailed inventory of assets and liabilities. This inventory provides a snapshot of financial status and helps identify which assets should be included in trusts, held jointly, or transferred through beneficiary deeds. Understanding debts and liabilities also ensures that sufficient resources are available to cover obligations before distributing assets to beneficiaries.

Defining Goals and Priorities

Each estate plan is as unique as the person creating it. By defining goals—such as providing for minor children, supporting a charitable cause, or ensuring business continuity—individuals can tailor their estate plan to reflect their values and intentions. Prioritizing specific assets or inheritance goals provides a strong foundation for selecting the most appropriate probate-free tools.

Consulting with an Estate Planning Attorney

Working with an experienced estate planning attorney can simplify the process, ensuring that all legal documents comply with Illinois probate laws and effectively bypass probate where possible. An attorney can help structure trusts, prepare wills, and offer guidance on combining joint tenancy, beneficiary deeds, and other tools for a comprehensive approach that aligns with personal goals.

Communicating the Plan with Family Members

Open communication about estate planning decisions helps set expectations and prevent future misunderstandings among beneficiaries. While each individual's level of transparency may vary, discussing key components—such as the roles of trustees or agents and the intent behind certain decisions—can ease the transition and provide reassurance to family members.

Reviewing and Updating the Plan Periodically

Life circumstances change, and estate plans should evolve accordingly. Major events like marriage, divorce, the birth of a child, or changes in financial status may affect inheritance goals or require updates to trusts and beneficiary designations. Reviewing the estate plan every few years, or after major life events, helps ensure it continues to meet family needs and avoids unintended consequences.

Final Thoughts: Proactive Estate Planning for Peace of Mind

Creating a comprehensive estate plan using probate-free tools like trusts, joint tenancy, and beneficiary deeds not only minimizes the probate process but also provides lasting security for families. By taking a proactive approach to planning, individuals can reduce stress for loved ones, prevent costly legal delays, and ensure that assets are managed according to their wishes. With the guidance of an estate planning attorney, readers can build an estate plan that reflects their values, protects their legacy, and provides clear direction for the future.

Summary

In Chapter 9, we explored strategies for avoiding probate and creating a thorough estate plan to simplify the inheritance process and protect loved ones. Here are the key takeaways:

1. **Trusts as a Probate Alternative**: A living trust allows individuals to place assets in a legal entity that bypasses probate, providing privacy, reducing costs, and giving beneficiaries quicker access to assets. Trusts also offer flexibility for complex inheritance plans and protection for minor or financially inexperienced heirs.

2. **Joint Tenancy and Beneficiary Deeds**: Joint tenancy and beneficiary deeds offer probate-free transfers of specific assets. Joint tenancy is ideal for shared property ownership, automatically passing to surviving owners, while beneficiary deeds allow for direct property transfer upon death without giving beneficiaries control during the owner's lifetime. Both options provide straightforward alternatives for certain assets, though they may not suit complex estate needs.

3. **Creating an Estate Plan**: A well-rounded estate plan combines probate-free tools with foundational elements like a will, powers of attorney, and healthcare directives. This proactive approach prevents family conflicts, reduces the burden on loved ones, and ensures assets are distributed according to personal wishes. Working with an estate planning attorney and regularly reviewing the plan ensures that it remains current and effective.

In summary, Chapter 9 emphasized the importance of comprehensive estate planning, with trusts, joint tenancy, and beneficiary deeds as probate-free options to consider. By creating an estate plan that aligns with individual goals, readers can reduce probate's impact on their families and provide lasting clarity, control, and peace of mind.

Checklist: Key Steps for Using Probate Alternatives in Estate Planning

1. Using Trusts as a Probate Alternative

- ☐ Determine if a living (revocable) trust is appropriate for your estate, as it allows assets to bypass probate and provides privacy and control.
- ☐ Work with an estate planning attorney to draft the trust document, specifying beneficiaries, terms, and instructions for asset management and distribution.
- ☐ Fund the trust by transferring assets, such as real estate, financial accounts, and valuable personal property, into the trust's name to ensure they are included.
- ☐ Designate a successor trustee who will manage the trust and distribute assets after your death, following your outlined wishes.
- ☐ Regularly review and update the trust to reflect life changes, such as the birth of children, divorce, or changes in financial status.

2. Setting Up Joint Tenancy for Probate-Free Property Transfers

- ☐ Consider joint tenancy with rights of survivorship for assets, such as real estate or bank accounts, if you wish for a specific person to inherit them automatically upon your passing.
- ☐ Understand that joint tenancy grants co-ownership rights, meaning all joint tenants have equal control and responsibility over the asset.
- ☐ Ensure that all joint tenants understand their rights and obligations, and consult a legal or tax professional if you're unsure about tax implications or other potential consequences.
- ☐ Keep clear records of any assets held in joint tenancy to simplify future estate planning and transfer processes.

3. Utilizing Beneficiary Deeds and Designations

- ☐ For real estate, consider using a beneficiary or transfer-on-death (TOD) deed to name a beneficiary who will inherit the property directly upon your death.

☐ File the beneficiary deed with the county recorder's office, and inform the named beneficiary about the designation to avoid confusion later.

☐ Review beneficiary designations on financial accounts, retirement plans, and life insurance policies, ensuring that they are accurate and up to date.

☐ Regularly check and update beneficiary designations, especially after major life changes, to make sure your intentions are accurately reflected.

4. Creating a Comprehensive Estate Plan

☐ Draft a last will and testament to address any assets not covered by trusts, joint tenancy, or beneficiary designations, and specify an executor to oversee your estate.

☐ Prepare a durable power of attorney to assign a trusted person to manage your financial and legal affairs in the event of your incapacity.

☐ Set up a healthcare directive or living will to outline your healthcare wishes if you become unable to communicate them yourself.

☐ Consult with an estate planning attorney to combine probate-free tools with traditional estate planning elements for a comprehensive and legally sound plan.

☐ Schedule periodic reviews of your estate plan to keep it current and relevant to your life circumstances, family dynamics, and any changes in Illinois probate law.

Chapter 10

Moving Forward with Confidence

Navigating probate and estate planning can seem overwhelming, especially during a time of loss or transition. But by understanding the probate process, exploring probate-free tools, and creating a comprehensive estate plan, readers can feel more prepared and empowered. In Illinois, where probate can be complex and time-consuming, taking proactive steps now can protect your assets and relieve stress for loved ones.

In this concluding chapter, we'll offer encouragement for moving forward, provide additional resources for further guidance, and extend an invitation to contact The Dick Barr Group for personalized support.

Encouragement and Resources: A Message from Dick Barr

To the readers who have made it through this guide—thank you for investing the time to understand probate and estate planning. I know that sorting through legal processes and inheritance decisions isn't easy, but every step you take now can make a lasting difference for you and your family. Whether you're working through probate as an executor or planning for the future of your own estate, you've already demonstrated a commitment to protecting your family's interests and securing their future.

Remember, probate and estate planning don't have to be journeys you navigate alone. Just as this book has provided you with knowledge, there are qualified professionals ready to help you every step of the way. From handling the sale of probate property to creating a customized estate plan, you don't have to take on these responsibilities by yourself. You're already on the right path to ensuring peace of mind for yourself and your loved ones.

At The Dick Barr Group, we bring access to some of the most respected, highly qualified resources available to assist you through every step of the probate process. From trusted property management services, repairs, cleaning, and maintenance to specialized professional services, we can connect you with skilled probate attorneys, tax advisors, CPAs, and tax attorneys, all experienced in Illinois probate matters. Our goal is to ensure that your family's legacy is handled with care, compassion, and expertise, leveraging a trusted network to meet your unique needs.

Additional Resources and Contacts

In addition to this guide, there are many resources available to Illinois residents that provide further assistance with probate and estate planning. Below are some resources that may be particularly helpful as you continue your journey:

- **Illinois Probate Courts**: Each county has its own probate court division. The Illinois Courts website (https://www.illinoiscourts.gov) offers links to county-specific probate resources, court forms, and contact information.

- **Illinois State Bar Association (ISBA)**: The ISBA offers educational materials, including articles on probate law, trusts, and estate planning. Visit their website at https://www.isba.org for more information.

- **Illinois Department of Revenue**: For questions on estate tax filing requirements or additional tax guidance, the Illinois Department of Revenue provides resources at https://www.revenue.illinois.gov.

- **Estate Planning Attorneys and Probate Specialists**: If you need help setting up a trust, creating a will, or managing probate complexities, reaching out to an Illinois estate planning attorney or probate specialist can provide expert guidance.

- **The Dick Barr Group**: As a Certified Probate Real Estate Specialist (C.P.R.S.), we specialize in handling probate real estate in Illinois, from property valuation and market analysis to sale negotiations. Our experienced team is here to support executors and families through every stage of the probate real estate process.

These resources offer additional guidance, helping you continue your probate and estate planning journey with reliable information and professional support.

Invitation to Reach Out

If you've found this guide helpful and would like personalized assistance, we at The Dick Barr Group are here for you. Probate can be a sensitive, complex process, and having the right support can make all the difference. Whether you have questions about managing a probate property sale, structuring an estate plan, or avoiding probate through strategic tools, we're ready to help.

We invite you to reach out to our team for a consultation tailored to your needs. At The Dick Barr Group, we take pride in guiding Illinois families through the intricacies of probate real estate, offering compassion, clarity, and expert solutions every step of the way. Please feel free to contact us to discuss how we can assist you with your unique situation.

Contact Information:

- **Phone**:   847.579.9736
- **Email**:   db@DickBarr.com
- **Website**:   www.DickBarr.com/probate-services

Thank you for allowing us to be part of your journey toward understanding and preparing for probate. Taking these steps now is an investment in your family's peace of mind, and we look forward to supporting you however we can.

Glossary of Probate Terms

Administrator

The person appointed by the probate court to manage and settle an estate when there is no will or when the named executor is unable to serve. An administrator has similar duties to an executor but is selected by the court.

Affidavit of Heirship

A legal document used when a person dies without a will. This affidavit establishes the legal heirs of the deceased, listing family members who are entitled to inherit. It is commonly used in real estate transactions to prove ownership in the absence of a will.

Beneficiary

An individual or entity designated in a will or other legal document to receive assets or property from an estate. Beneficiaries can include family members, friends, charities, or other organizations.

Certified Copy

An official, authenticated copy of a document, such as a death certificate or will, that proves its legitimacy. Certified copies are often required in probate for actions like transferring titles or accessing accounts.

Codicil

An amendment or addition to an existing will, used to make minor changes without creating a new will. A codicil must meet the same legal standards as the original will to be valid.

Creditor's Claim

A formal request for payment made by a creditor to the estate for debts owed by the decedent. Illinois probate law requires creditors to submit claims within a specific time frame, usually within six months after notice is given to creditors.

Decedent

The legal term for the person who has passed away and whose estate is being administered in probate. Probate is the process of distributing the decedent's assets and settling any remaining debts.

Deed

A legal document that establishes ownership of real estate. In probate, deeds are used to transfer property titles to heirs, beneficiaries, or buyers if the property is sold.

Estate

The total property, assets, and debts left by an individual at the time of death. An estate includes real estate, personal property, bank accounts, investments, and other financial assets.

Executor

The person named in a will to administer the decedent's estate, including paying debts, distributing assets, and ensuring the will's provisions are fulfilled. In Illinois, the executor must be formally appointed by the probate court.

Fiduciary Duty

A legal obligation to act in the best interests of another party. Executors, administrators, and other fiduciaries have a duty to act responsibly and honestly on behalf of the estate and its beneficiaries.

Heir

A person who is legally entitled to inherit property or assets from an estate when there is no will. Illinois intestate succession laws determine the order of heirs, typically starting with the closest family members.

Intestate

A term describing a situation in which a person dies without a valid will. In such cases, the estate is distributed according to Illinois intestate succession laws, which prioritize spouses, children, and other close relatives.

Intestate Succession

The legal process that determines who inherits property when someone dies without a will. In Illinois, intestate succession follows a specific order: typically, the spouse and children first, then extended family members if no immediate family exists.

Letters of Office (Letters Testamentary)

Official documents issued by the probate court that authorize the executor or administrator to act on behalf of the estate. These letters allow access to accounts, the ability to transfer property, and the authority to handle other estate matters.

Liability

An outstanding debt or obligation of the estate, including mortgages, loans, credit card debts, or unpaid bills. Liabilities must be paid before distributing any assets to beneficiaries.

Life Estate

A type of property ownership where an individual has the right to use or live in a property for the duration of their life. After the individual's death, the property typically passes to a remainder beneficiary.

Notice to Creditors

A formal notification given to creditors by the executor or administrator, informing them of the decedent's death and the opportunity to file claims against the estate within a specified time frame.

Personal Property

All property other than real estate, including belongings such as jewelry, cars, artwork, and household goods. Personal property may be distributed to heirs as specified in the will or according to Illinois intestate laws.

Petition for Probate

The initial filing document submitted to the probate court to officially begin the probate process. This petition requests the court to recognize the decedent's will (if one exists) and appoint an executor or administrator.

Power of Attorney
A legal document authorizing one person to act on behalf of another in financial or healthcare matters. Note that a power of attorney becomes void upon the death of the individual who granted it; probate is then required to manage the estate.

Probate
The legal process by which a court supervises the distribution of a decedent's estate, ensuring debts are paid, and assets are distributed according to the will or state laws if no will exists.

Probate Assets
Assets owned solely by the decedent that require probate court oversight to transfer ownership. Examples include individual bank accounts, real estate solely owned by the decedent, and personal belongings.

Real Property
Land and anything permanently attached to it, such as buildings or structures. Real property in probate may include the decedent's primary residence, rental properties, and other types of real estate.

Residue (Residuary Estate)
The remaining portion of the estate after debts, taxes, and specific bequests have been distributed. The residue is typically distributed to residuary beneficiaries named in the will or to heirs if no will exists.

Small Estate Affidavit
A simplified procedure for administering an estate without going through formal probate, available in Illinois when the total estate value is below a certain threshold. This affidavit allows heirs to collect and transfer certain assets more quickly.

Testate
A term describing a situation in which a person dies with a valid will. In testate probate, the estate is distributed according to the provisions in the will.

Trust
A legal arrangement where assets are held by a trustee for the benefit of specific individuals or organizations. Assets in a trust generally avoid probate, as they are distributed directly to the named beneficiaries.

Will
A legal document specifying how an individual wants their property and assets distributed upon their death. A valid will also names an executor to administer the estate and may include guardianship preferences for minor children.

Will Contest

A formal challenge to the validity of a will, typically based on claims such as undue influence, lack of mental capacity, or improper execution. Will contests are handled by the probate court and can impact the distribution of the estate.

Acknowledgments

This book represents a culmination of countless hours, hard work, and the unwavering support of people who believed in me and in this mission to help families navigate the probate real estate process.

To my coach, Chris Fox: thank you for pushing me beyond my limits, challenging me to grow, and guiding me through both the highs and lows of this journey. Your mentorship has been instrumental in shaping not only my career, but also my understanding of the impact I want to make for families facing difficult transitions.

To my team at The Dick Barr Group, Christin, Danielle, Angel, Ken, I'm deeply grateful for each of you. Every client we've served, every problem we've solved, and every step we've taken to refine our expertise in probate real estate is because of your commitment and dedication. Thank you for your relentless drive and the heart you bring to our work.

To my broker at Village Realty, Bob Linke, I owe a debt of gratitude for providing me with a foundation of support, guidance, and professionalism. Your leadership has been invaluable, allowing me to grow and build a business I'm truly proud of.

And most importantly, to my wife, Holly—none of this would have been possible without you. You've sacrificed so much and supported me unconditionally, allowing me to chase my dreams and build a business centered around helping others. Thank you for your patience, your love, and your belief in me. Your strength and encouragement have been the foundation of everything I do, and I'm endlessly grateful for your partnership on this journey.

To all of you—this book is as much yours as it is mine. Thank you for being an essential part of this mission.

About the Author

Dick Barr is a highly respected Managing Broker with The Dick Barr Group at Village Realty, specializing in residential real estate in Illinois, with an emphasis on serving families in Lake, McHenry and Cook Counties. With years of expertise guiding clients through the often complex and emotional landscape of probate real estate, Dick brings a unique blend of technical knowledge, compassion, and community dedication to each transaction. He understands that dealing with a loved one's estate involves more than just property management—it's a deeply personal journey, often fraught with challenges. By focusing on clarity, respect, and diligent support, Dick has become a trusted ally for families navigating this difficult process.

Dick's comprehensive understanding of Illinois probate law as it relates to real estate, is rooted in years of practice and certifications in probate real estate. He has an in-depth command of Illinois Probate Statute Article VI and other legal requirements specific to probate sales and property management. Known for his ability to demystify complex legal and real estate processes, Dick offers families the confidence and direction they need to manage their probate real estate with peace of mind.

In addition to his role as Managing Broker, Dick has served as an elected Lake County Board Member and Forest Preserve Commissioner. His public service has given him a deep commitment to his community and an understanding of local governance and property concerns that further informs his approach to real estate. He leverages his community insights to provide families with a seamless experience, whether they're handling property transfers, dealing with probate court, or selling estate assets.

With a technological approach to real estate, Dick utilizes cutting-edge tools to deliver quality service, ensuring each property is marketed and managed to its full potential. This forward-thinking approach, combined with his dedication to accuracy and empathetic guidance, has set Dick and The Dick Barr Group apart as leading probate real estate professionals in Illinois.

Dick's passion for helping families through probate extends beyond business. He believes in empowering his clients with knowledge and clear communication, offering them not only a practical guide but a sense of stability during a challenging time. His commitment to client education and advocacy has made him a sought-after voice in Illinois probate real estate, and his work is driven by a deep desire to make the process manageable, dignified, and ultimately successful for the families he serves.

URGENT PLEA!

Thank You For Reading My Book!
I really appreciate all of your feedback and
I love hearing what you have to say.

I need your input to make the next version of this
book (and my future books) better.

Please take two minutes now to leave a helpful
review on Amazon letting me know what you
thought of the book.

Thanks so much!

—Dick Barr